Modern Chrysler Concept Cars

The designs that saved the company

Matt DeLorenzo

MBI Publishing Company

First published in 2000 by MBI Publishing Company,
729 Prospect Avenue, PO Box 1, Osceola, WI 54020-0001 USA

MBI Publishing Company books are also available at discounts in bulk quantity for industrial or sales-promotional use. For details write to Special Sales Manager at Motorbooks International Wholesalers & Distributors, 729 Prospect Avenue, PO Box 1, Osceola WI, 54020 USA.

Edited by Steve Hendrickson

Designed by Arthur Durkee

Printed in China

Library of Congress Cataloging-in-Publication Data
DeLorenzo, Matt.
    Modern Chrysler concept cars: the designs that saved the company /
Matthew S. DeLorenzo.
        p. cm.—(MBI Publishing Company Colortech)
    Includes index.
    ISBN 0-7603-0848-9 (pbk. : alk. paper)
    1. Chrysler automobile—Design and construction.
2. Experimental automobiles 3. Chrysler Corporation.
I. Title. II. Series.
    TL215.C55 D45 2000   2000
    629.2'31—dc21   00-0029183

On the front cover: The Chrysler Atlantic, conceived by Tom Gale and Bob Lutz to pay homage to classic French coachbuilders, is retro design at its finest. Unlike most previous concept cars, the Atlantic was built to be driven. *John Lamm*

On the frontispiece: Inspired by the Viper's racing successes, the Viper GTS-R concept sports a huge rear wing, front aerodynamic splitter, and roof air intake, taking the already radical Viper several steps further. *John Lamm*

On the title page: The Pronto Cruizer looks right at home outside a vintage diner. *Bill Delaney*

On the back cover: The Pronto Cruizer was conceived as an American hot rod draped around a European hatchback, and was Chrysler's first concept car launched in Europe since the Portofino in 1987. This design led to the production version of PT Cruiser. *Bill Delaney*

CONTENTS

ACKNOWLEDGMENTS 6

INTRODUCTION 7

CHAPTER ONE TOO GOOD TO WASTE 9

CHAPTER TWO DREAM CARS MATTER 27

CHAPTER THREE LH MEANS MORE THAN LAST HOPE 35

CHAPTER FOUR PERFORMANCE RULES 49

CHAPTER FIVE AN ICON FOR CHRYSLER 65

CHAPTER SIX SEARCHING FOR A PERFECT JEEP 77

CHAPTER SEVEN TECHNOLOGY RULES 91

CHAPTER EIGHT FUTURE STARS 99

CHAPTER NINE CONCEPTS WITH A CONSCIENCE 107

CHAPTER TEN FROM CONCEPT TO REALITY 123

EPILOGUE DAIMLERCHRYSLER DAYS 137

INDEX 144

ACKNOWLEDGMENTS

This book represents the cumulative efforts of many people who contributed their time and unique talents to make it happen. As with any work that casts a look behind the scenes, the cooperation of the principals involved is crucial. My sincere thanks go to Tom Gale, DaimlerChrysler executive vice president of product development and design, who found time in his hectic schedule to sit down for a series of interviews. Also, I greatly appreciate the insights of former Chrysler executives Bob Lutz and Francois Castaing.

The DaimlerChrysler design staff was extremely helpful in pulling together sketches and adding additional information. My thanks go to John Herlitz, Neil Walling, and Trevor Creed. I'd also like to add a personal thanks to Public Relations Vice President Steve Rossi, who was key in getting this project off the ground.

Scott Fosgard and Sjoerd Dijkstra, also from DaimlerChrysler public relations, were extremely helpful in arranging interviews and combing company archives for past press kits and photography. This story would be nothing without pictures of the cars, and fortunately, I was able to obtain the best photography in the business from John Lamm and Bill Delaney.

I could not have completed this project without the support and understanding of everyone at my day job at *Road & Track*, especially Editor-in-Chief Thos Bryant.

Last, but certainly not least, I'd like to thank my family: Amy and Stephen for being patient while Dad was locked away in his office, and especially my partner and copy editor, Jane, for her painstaking attention to detail, and most of all for her understanding.
—*Matt DeLorenzo*

INTRODUCTION

Concept cars are the stars of the auto show circuit. Nothing gathers crowds faster than these shiny visions of the future. Cynics may dismiss concept cars as publicity stunts to spruce up a show stand populated by everyday cars and trucks that look like every other vehicle. The manufacturers themselves are somewhat to blame for that cynicism. Historically, production models have been a far cry from the zoomy looks promised by some concepts.

It is natural for the auto companies to want their designers and engineers to dream. It's the spark of creativity offered by designing show cars that provides relief to the people caught up in the difficult work of developing ordinary cars and trucks. Working on a concept car gives the designer the unique opportunity to start with a clean sheet of paper; unencumbered by budgets, production feasibility, or available technology. Often when the costs, reality of assembly, and components that exist in a company's parts bin are cranked into the equation, some of the show cars are impossible to produce. The dream car becomes an ice sculpture slowly melting away in the harsh daylight of reality.

At least that was the way it used to work. In the 1990s, almost out of desperation, Chrysler virtually rewrote the book on how auto manufacturers view and use show cars. The basics were the same: allow the designers and engineers to stretch a bit, play "what if?", discover new niches, and develop new technology. It was a chance to obtain free publicity for a company where "cash-strapped" and "ailing" seemed to be part of its name.

Even though the company was struggling, Chrysler invested in a series of show cars that pointed in the direction of future product lines. But better yet, it made a commitment to faithfully reproduce concepts cars the public could buy. It was a way to send the message Chrysler wasn't going down without a fight. These cars would demonstrate that although sales were sliding, a turnaround was in the air. The bold styling statements proclaimed this was a company that was in the car business and that had exciting products in the pipeline—if the employees, investment community, and customers would continue to support it.

The idea of creating show cars and actually producing them didn't just happen. It evolved over a period of time beginning back in the late 1980s when Chrysler, having been saved by government loan guarantees at the beginning of the decade, was losing its steam. A unique set of circumstances—the acquisition of AMC and its cadre of can-do executives, the hiring of Robert Lutz, and the gelling of a capable design staff under Chrysler veteran Tom Gale—drew together a product team that comes along only once in a generation. This is how that group redefined the concept car for an industry and, in the process, saved Chrysler.

CHAPTER ONE

TOO GOOD TO WASTE

Chrysler's incredible run of attention-getting show cars started with a cast-off that was gathering dust in a back room of the company's Pacifica Design Studio in Carlsbad, California. It was a design too good to waste.

Tom Gale, vice president of design, had soldiered on long enough, designing square boxes with vinyl roofs and fake wire wheels while taking orders from the market research types who insisted that their clinics proved the beltline should be a quarter-inch higher.

It was time for the designers "to do one for ourselves," Gale recalls. That "one" would be the Navaho. Gale had an idea for a radical approach to sedan design called cab forward. It meant maximizing the passenger cabin by minimizing the distance between the base of the windshield and the front wheels. Really aggressive cab forward designs would have that touchdown point over the centerline of the front wheel. In addition to providing more interior space, cab forward required a more steeply raked, wind-cheating windshield to achieve its objective. In the mid-1980s, it was a far more radical approach to styling than Ford's highly praised and standard-setting aerodynamic Taurus and Sable. While these cars had clean, rounded shapes, the basic architecture itself was conventional. Cab forward involved a whole new proportion, and Navaho embodied this new philosophy.

But this was 1985 and Gale couldn't sell the shape to upper management. So Navaho was consigned to storage in the Pacifica studio.

This was a period of great uncertainty at Chrysler. Though Chairman Lee Iacocca had, with great fanfare, repaid the last of the government-backed loans that helped bail the company out of near bankruptcy in the early 1980s, Chrysler's future was by no means assured.

Even Iacocca later admitted that he took his eye off the ball when the company used profits from booming sales, which rose from just over $1 million at the low point in 1981 to nearly $2 million by 1986, to diversify. This

Portofino was a running prototype built in Turin, Italy. Later, while it was being transported in the United States, the semi-truck it was riding in overturned. The nearly destroyed show car was completely restored by Metalcrafters, a Southern California coachbuilder that produces the bulk of Chrysler's concepts.
John Lamm

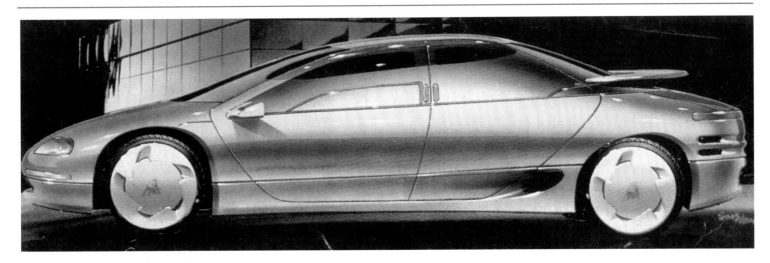

Early sketches of the Portofino show two basic design elements far different from anything Chrysler was putting on the road in the 1980s. The front windshield was steeply raked and touched down nearly at the centerline of the front wheel, while the rear end kicked up or "gestured." *Chrysler*

diversification drive saw the company jump into financial services, defense contracting, and even executive aircraft with the purchase of Gulfstream Aviation. Along the way, Chrysler also acquired Automobili Lamborghini and American Motors Corporation (AMC) in 1987 (and its coveted Jeep brand), briefly boosting sales to 2.3 million cars and trucks.

Iacocca believed the new non-automotive interests would protect Chrysler during the next downturn in the car market. Instead, these businesses drained needed resources away from the core business of building vehicles—money desperately needed to refresh its aging, K-platform-based cars and minivans. The company had used every trick in the book to disguise this one-platform-fits-all approach.

"If nothing else, we were masters of illusion," says John Herlitz, Gale's right-hand-man. "The Dodge Dynasty rode on a wheelbase that was actually one inch shorter than today's Neon. And, when there was no other way to effectively renew the basic body shell, we resorted to all the tricks that a self-respecting designer would run and hide from. We had padded vinyl roofs, opera windows, chrome tiara roof moldings, fake wire wheels, whitewall tires, huge chrome bodyside moldings, and on and on."

Even as Chrysler was gobbling up other companies, the wheels were starting to come off. Just after the AMC acquisition, Wall Street sent out the message that Chrysler was in big trouble. Sales began a slide that would bottom out in 1991 at 1.5 million units.

Even though the 1980s were a time of tremendous turmoil at Chrysler, the seeds for its turnaround were being planted. In 1986, Robert A. Lutz joined Chrysler as president after stints at Ford, GM, Opel, and BMW. Though Lutz, like Iacocca, worked on the marketing side, unlike Iacocca, the ex-Marine aviator wore his enthusiasm for cars on his sleeve. While Iacocca toyed with the idea of being president of the United States, Lutz toyed with his collection of cars, motorcycles, and airplanes. Along with the AMC merger came a group of executives who were used to adversity and working on shoestring budgets. There were strong product development executives like Francois Castaing and public relations professionals like Steve Harris and Tom Kowaleski, who recognized the value of product in promoting a company.

Chrysler's management, including its PR staff, had been through the financial crisis wringer of the late 1970s and early 1980s and was highly skilled at working with the government and Wall Street in order to assure the company's survival. By contrast, Harris and Kowaleski, trained in the school of doing more with less at AMC, had the

uncanny knack of launching vehicles in a way that garnered maximum publicity.

This new blood was focused on using product as the means to lift the company out of the doldrums. They found a kindred spirit in Tom Gale, a Chrysler veteran who headed product design. Gale had been offered jobs at both General Motors and Chrysler when he graduated from Michigan State in 1967, but chose the latter because it offered him an opportunity to do some engineering first

Since Portofino would be badged as a Lamborghini, Chrysler designers felt free to use scissors-style doors. *Chrysler*

Though Portofino wore Lamborghini's charging bull, the blacked-out C-pillar and sweep of the rear window would be used later on the Dodge Intrepid sedan. *John Lamm*

rather than just straight design. It was a difficult decision for the Flint native, who grew up in a GM family and interned with the company during his schooling. Gale worked for four years in body engineering before moving over to the design staff in 1972.

For awhile, it must have seemed like the wrong decision. In 1974, Gale was sent home for the Thanksgiving holidays. While the water cooler talk said the designers would be out through Christmas, it wasn't until April 1975 that they were called back to work. Gale says that while he never looks back, he admits he always admired GM design.

"I admired them because the designers had absolute power," Gale says. "They always had absolute influence over package and architecture. At Chrysler, we had always been, as an office, reactive. Someone would come to us and give us an assignment and tell us what to do. We never really had a chance to say, 'Well, have you considered this?' They'd say, 'No, we're out of time and we're out of money and we have to do this.' Basically design was reactive instead of proactive. We were never in a position to go for it. If we didn't change radically, we would never get out in front."

Lutz, Castaing, and Gale would be the three legs that supported Chrysler's new way of using concept cars. Though they didn't necessarily see eye-to-eye on everything, they were able to work toward turning around Chrysler's image.

Gale was keeper of the flame, the guy who pushed the idea of resurrecting Chrysler's pure performance image from its muscle car heyday. He was different from other designers in that he not only spoke the pure design vocabulary of form and proportion, but he had a practical mechanical bent to this thinking, thanks to his stint as a body engineer and his passion for tinkering with cars.

If Gale kept the flame, Lutz stoked the bonfire. He was the big picture guy, the visionary who wanted cars that made grand statements about Chrysler, not just as an American icon, but as a global player. The Swiss-born

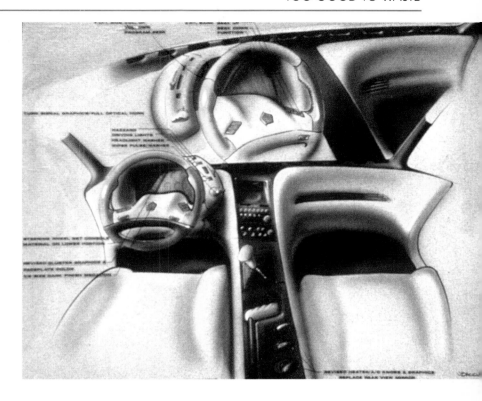

The interior concept called for a dual cockpit arrangement separated by a large console running the entire length of the passenger cabin. *Chrysler*

Lutz viewed Chrysler from his perspective as a European who grew up knowing that Briggs Cunningham's Le Mans racers and Peter Monteverdi's world-beating executive sedans relied on Chrysler Hemi power. He also appreciated the fact that the Chrysler Imperials of the 1930s could go toe-to-toe with the European grand classics from the same era. It was Lutz who wanted the world to know that Chrysler understood these traditions, from his insistence that they do concepts like the Atlantic and Phaeton to taking on and winning Le Mans with the Viper GTS Coupe.

The center console from the early sketches is faithfully executed in the show car. *John Lamm*

From any angle, the Portofino's upward swinging doors are an impressive sight. Gas struts were used to support their weight. *John Lamm*

Castaing was the pure engineer. He ran Renault's Formula One racing team before coming to AMC when the French company took a 49-percent stake in the American company. Steeped in advanced technology, Castaing insisted on infusing show cars with technology to show that Chrysler could develop new approaches that not only provided transportation but also solved some of the problems inherent in mass automobility.

Unlike other companies, where concept cars were more often than not the province of design staff, the responsibility for developing show cars was spread among top management. The dynamics among these three at Chrysler would prove critical to the evolution of the concept car from flashy showstopper to a valuable communication and product development medium. It wasn't just about design, but rather image, technology, and most

importantly, the viability of the company. And these messages were sent to a wide audience—the public, the press, Wall Street, and especially to Chrysler employees battered by pay cuts, hiring freezes, and benefit rollbacks.

But first, Chrysler needed a process to bring these concepts to life. As the cash temporarily rolled in during the mid-1980s, the company opened its Pacifica Design Studio in California, with great fanfare. Japanese imports were riding high and were trumpeting the successes of their California design studios. Almost overnight,

European manufacturers and the U.S. Big Three had to have a presence in the Golden State. Gale used this opportunity to reorganize his staff and assign Pacifica to work on advanced design.

"I took about a third of the resources and devoted them to packaging and advanced design and took a look at where we wanted to go with programs," Gale says. "The whole bet was that if we did a good job in advanced design, the job in between—getting the car from concept to production—would be easier."

Getting the backing of upper management to do a full-blown concept car and taking it to production was another matter altogether. "We did a few furtive show cars, but they weren't concept cars by any definition. But they were significant in that we were developing a process to do them."

The first concept car to start Chrysler down this long path was the Portofino, which got its start in 1985 as that Pacifica study.

Enter Bob Lutz. "What became the Portofino was there when I got there," Lutz recalls. "I saw that at my first

visit to Pacifica and it was called the Navaho. It was a wood armature, fiberglass inside and outside, and it was roughly the Portofino's shape. It wasn't planned for any powertrain and I said, 'Wow, look at that thing.' I was stunned. Tom Gale told me that he did that study to explore alternate shapes of what we could do if we packaged the powertrain differently. I wanted to investigate it further, but he said it was dead, that Chrysler didn't have any powertrain that could be credibly packaged."

Gale also didn't have any budget to do the car. But Lutz did, as head of international operations. At the time, Chrysler was looking to expand its presence in Europe as well as trying to leverage Iacocca's Lamborghini

Millennium was a pure design exercise to test the absolute limits of cab forward architecture, while still being able to package a 3.0-liter front-drive V-6 in the vehicle. Design chief Tom Gale says that if you look straight down on the car, you can't tell which is the front or the rear. *Chrysler*

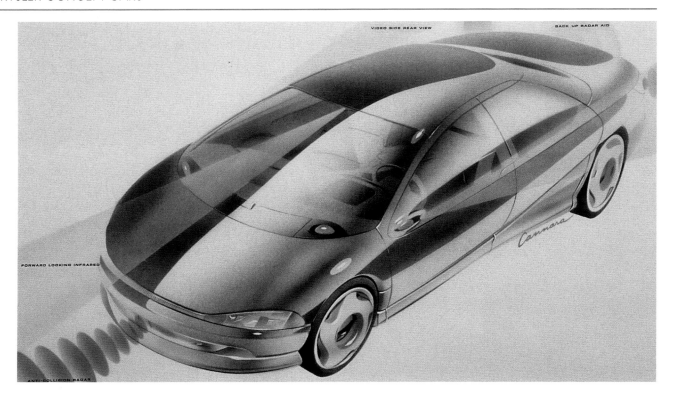

In addition to selling the idea of cab forward to the public, Millennium also demonstrated advanced safety features like forward looking radar and infrared night vision as well as production-ready technologies like traction control and anti-lock brakes. *Chrysler*

acquisition. It was decided that the Navaho could accommodate a Lamborghini Jalpa V-8 mounted amidships.

With Portofino, Gale says: "We would kill three birds with one stone. First, it would reintroduce Chrysler into Europe, give us something for Lamborghini to show, and do a design that foreshadowed the Dodge LH. If you look closely at the car, you'll see all the graphics were a precursor for the Intrepid. And that was really the beginning of cab forward. It fit the proportion we had been sketching anyway."

The four doors on the Portofino swung up from the center of the car, much like the scissors-action doors on the Countach and its replacement, the Diablo.

The car had some unique design features. There was no B-pillar, and both the hood and rear deck opened clamshell style. Inside, the instrument pod, steering wheel, and pedals were fully adjustable to the driver's position, while the four-passenger interior was clad in hand-sewn leather. The press materials boasted that the 3.5-liter V-8, which was rated at 225 horsepower at 7,000 rpm and

229 ft-lb of torque at 3,500 rpm, was capable of propelling the vehicle to a top speed of more than 150 miles per hour. The V-8 was also teamed with Lamborghini's own five-speed manual. The Portofino rode on an independent front and rear suspension with McPherson struts, coil springs, and ventilated disc brakes front and rear.

But most important was the shape. It was the first public showing of cab forward architecture.

"Portofino was a stunning show car," Lutz says. "The shape, the color, the noble Lamborghini twin cam powertrain. It was magic. You look at it today and it still looks great. Thematically, it contained so much we later used. The sweep around the backlight we used on Intrepid.

"But Portofino had another enormously important function," Lutz continues. "We still had Lee Iacocca around, and he had extremely conservative taste. He liked,

just like Henry Ford II, cars with a waterline belt. The beltline had to be absolutely horizontal. He didn't like anything wedge shaped. He didn't like anything with a curved beltline. Whenever we showed anything with a diving hood or a lot of gesture to it, he didn't like it, because in his programming, that didn't radiate luxury or power. If we had proposed cab forward production cars without conditioning our CEO with the Portofino, we would have never been able to sell the LH line to him. We would have wound up with something more conservative.

"Remember, this was the guy who, when I joined Chrysler, told me I was joining at a good time because Ford had made a fatal mistake with the Taurus. He said all of Chrysler research indicated the Taurus was going to be a hopeless flop because they got 5 on a 10-point scale, whereas Chrysler's new stuff, the C-body Dynasty and

Long before Viper, Chrysler president Hal Sperlich had a vision for three sports cars: Big Shot, Hot Shot, and Sling Shot. This is Sling Shot, designed by Craig Durfey, who also penned the Viper. He was assisted by a group of Chrysler design interns. Unlike future concept cars, this one didn't run. *Chrysler*

The 1987 Dodge Intrepid, also known as Big Shot, while it carried the same name as the future LH sedan, was really a design exercise used to develop the shape of the Dodge Stealth and Mitsubishi 3000GT, both of which were built in Japan. *Chrysler*

New Yorker averaged 7.5. The problem was, the 5s that Taurus ran were an average of half the population giving it 9s and 10s and half giving it 1s and 2s. That's how you win in this business. The 7.5s meant the Chryslers were everyone's second choice and no one sells second choices anywhere. So he was convinced the Taurus was going to flop and couldn't understand why it did so well and why we had to rebate the C-bodies almost right off the bat.

"Once he started getting up on the podium with Portofino and hearing all the favorable comments, it became his car," Lutz laughs. "Then Tom Gale and I started hearing from him. 'We've got to figure out a way to make the production stuff look like Portofino,' he'd say. And that's when we knew we moved the last of the obstacles."

Before Iacocca was convinced that Portofino was Chrysler's future, Gale had begun work on the Millennium. This car would explore the limits of the new cab forward architecture.

"I wanted to see if we used Portofino as a starting point, how far we could go," Gale explains. "Millennium was a test to see to what extreme could we take it. The brief called for a car of about 3.0-liters, and it had to be a V-6 and front-drive. It was our next proportional study on a plausible platform and it was pretty interesting. I've shown just a top view of the Millennium and you don't realize how extreme the cab forward really is on that car. You can't tell the front from the back when you look straight down at it."

Extreme it was. Millennium measured 194.7 inches in overall length and the wheelbase was 122 inches. Lutz recalls that Millennium was done in back rooms outside Highland Park under the guise of a possible new project for Alejandro DeTomaso, who was involved in building the Chrysler TC Coupe by Maserati.

"He [DeTomaso] was always looking for new ways to have Chrysler fund his ventures," Lutz says. "What he really wanted to do was bring back the Maserati Quattroporte with a big hairy four-cam V-8 engine. If we did that, it would make a hell of a lot more sense than the TC Coupe, especially if it would have a fully unique body, gorgeous, real Italian interior instead of fake, real noble powertrain, and a modern, sharply gestured European shape but more of an American size. I knew it was never going to work out financially, but I was enthused to have Tom go off and do a clay model on it.

"When we looked at the clay model, even before it had windows cut in, we said, 'What are we going to do with this thing? It will never be a Maserati. We'll just finish it up and hide it someplace.'"

It was too good to waste. Later, when the way was cleared for cab forward, Chrysler took the Millennium out to show the public. In addition to signaling a future design direction, Millennium was executed as a demonstration in advanced safety features. It began a pattern of loading show cars with future technology or "surprise and delight" features that might be incorporated in future models. By doing so, it made the cars more real and gave the company other story lines beyond design.

The cockpit of the Viper show car has a spare, race car feel to it. Adding to the aura are aluminum-drilled foot pedals, the three-spoke steering wheel, and the baseball-stitched shift knob. *John Lamm*

The Millennium was loaded with a mix of ideas, some destined for production, others mere fantasy. A functional group of features, called "safety through control," included traction control, active suspension, four-wheel anti-lock brakes, and voice-activated controls. A second group was characterized as "safety through visibility," which relied on head-up navigation, forward-looking infrared vision for night and fog conditions, rain-sensitive wipers, and a heated windshield. A third grouping of technology called "safety through warnings" included blind-spot radar, which would set off an audible tone, back-up warning, collision warning radar, and warnings for low tire inflation, low brake pad, and brake fluid. It also included a device that could detect alcohol on the breath of the

The Viper show car's engine was cobbled together by adding cylinders to an existing V-8. Lamborghini would develop an aluminum block based on the V-10 being designed for Chrysler's Ram pickup. *John Lamm*

driver and automatically disable the car. The final complement of equipment was called "safety through protection." It featured air bags, rear-seat head restraints, a specially designed child safety seat, on-board navigation, and an anti-theft security system.

In retrospect, it's readily apparent that the LH had its roots in the Portofino and Millennium design studies. But at the time there were few outside the company who knew what Chrysler was up to, or actually believed that the company would risk its declining fortunes on such avant-garde designs. Something more dramatic was needed to convince Wall Street and the press that genuine change was under way at Chrysler. That something was Viper.

The idea of doing a sports car was nothing new at Chrysler. Hal Sperlich, who left Ford to join Chrysler in the 1970s and is credited with creating the minivan, pushed an idea to do three sports cars. One was called Big Shot, a 1987 mid-engine study on a Daytona platform, ironically named Intrepid, which would spawn the Dodge Stealth/Mitsubishi 3000GT. The second, called Hot Shot, explored the idea of doing a Jeep-based sports car, but it was an idea that was quickly abandoned. The third was Sling Shot, a small, two-seat open car that was eventually built with the help of interns and shown in 1988.

Big Shot "was designed to re-establish Chrysler or Dodge on the top of the performance heap," Lutz recalls. "But my point was you can't do it with a badge-engineered captive import. If it isn't your own idea, your own technology, and your own fabrication, no one will give you credit for it. And that's why I think the Stealth never did much for us in terms of image."

After a routine strategy meeting in February 1988, Lutz asked Gale to visit his office where he proposed doing a modern Cobra. Lutz had just gotten an Autokraft Mark IV Cobra and was toying with the idea of replacing the Ford engine with a Chrysler 360, even though it produces about 150 less horsepower. But, at the time, he knew a cast-iron 488-ci V-10 was coming for the Ram pickup, along with a five-speed manual. Then he also thought about beefing up the rear end with Dakota truck components. After thinking it through, Lutz was convinced that Chrysler, by using truck parts, could build a big hairy sports car that would give the company a much-needed shot of adrenaline.

"It's true the Viper idea came out of discussions with Carroll Shelby and Bob Lutz, but Bob was unaware that a lot of stuff was going on down in the studio," Gale remembers. "A few weeks later, I invited him over, had half-size packages of the vehicle with a sports car layout, and laid it out with the sketches. He was a great champion for this stuff. But not another word was said. We just had a great reaction from him and he finished the walk-through. Three weeks later, we had an offsite and showed him the first clay model. But he wasn't necessarily blown away. He didn't like the front end of the car."

Lutz admits: "I didn't like it at first. Those sketches were very close to the car now. In my mind's eye, I wanted something closer to the Cobra, more literal in interpretation." But as the project progressed, Lutz warmed to the new shape.

"The more I saw, the more we started doing in clay, the more I knew it was going to be dynamite," Lutz says. "It's interesting that the Viper went the opposite way of most concept cars in that the first car was done in metal and then the production car was plastic. Usually, it works the other way."

While the Viper's existence is generally credited to the work of the "fourfathers"—Shelby, Lutz, Gale, and Castaing—their work was actually done in series rather than a team effort. Shelby had those initial conversations with Lutz, but because of Shelby's heart transplant, didn't really play an active role in the development of the car. Gale, Neil Walling, and Craig Durfey (who actually penned the Viper) did the design and worked with Metal-crafters, a small California coachbuilder, to produce the show car. Francois Castaing was instrumental in getting the vehicle into production by assembling the platform

While side pipes did make it into production, unfortunately, the graceful headers, which were partially exposed with the hood down, didn't. *John Lamm*

team under Roy Sjoberg and using the components and resources of Jeep and truck engineering.

"Francois deserves all the credit in the world for getting the team established and getting the Viper going down the road," Gale says.

Lutz agrees, noting that the car-engineering group would "come up with a million reasons why we shouldn't be doing this, that the capacity of engineers was stretched to the limit. I wanted to keep it a truck project because most of the hardware was truck."

As a show car, the Viper was an immediate hit. It took only three months from the unveiling at the 1989 North American International Auto Show to get the official go-ahead from the Chrysler board. While the production car looks like the show car, upon closer inspection, it's apparent that they are quite different in execution. Several of the unique design features—the windshield that appears to float above the cowl and the headers poking out of the side vents—clearly were not feasible in the production car. An aluminum mill developed with the assistance of Lamborghini supplanted the cast-iron V-10, which was built by adding two more cylinders onto the 360-ci V-8 block.

"The final car is better than the concept car," Gale says. "We protected all the imagery and yet there isn't a surface on the car that is the same, though a bystander probably couldn't see a hell of a lot of difference between the two cars."

The Viper sent the message that it wasn't business as usual at Chrysler. "The Viper's larger contribution was to show that we weren't going down without a fight," Lutz says. "I loved the outrage of a company that was going out of business, that people wondered why couldn't we die with dignity as opposed to thrashing about like this, and suddenly, we were showing a Viper with an 8.0-liter V-10 engine and an announced 400 horsepower."

And the Viper was built as a runner. "You have to deliver on a few things so that people can't dismiss the car out of hand," Gale notes. "I've always said, we may not do many concept cars, but the ones I do, I'm going to make them so I can drive them. That's why we make them out of metal."

The Viper pointed Chrysler concept cars in a new direction. "We found out we could explore the limits of how much is enough and how much is too much when you start to look at elements of trend and style," Gale explains. "And not only do they energize everybody, energize management, and show Wall Street—who said, 'Wow, you guys are alive'—but they build a reputation for your office and your company. When we took the cover off the Viper, no one else was doing things that were inspired by the past. You stake out a little bit of turf that makes it that much tougher for someone to come in. You start to put pressure on others to reach a little further or maybe they do something goofy. They're going to react and as soon as they're reactive, that means you're in the lead."

The Viper signaled that Chrysler was done playing defense. It was going on offense.

From any angle, the Viper projects a powerful presence,
precisely what the doctor ordered to rejuvenate the
Dodge brand. *John Lamm*

CHAPTER TWO

DREAM CARS MATTER

Chrysler didn't invent the show car. It merely took a good idea and evolved it into an art form. Manufacturers have been wowing the public with dream cars since the first one, the 1938 Buick Y-Job. Legendary GM design chief Harley Earl wanted to build a car that projected his vision for the future of automotive design—longer, lower, wider. The Y-Job accomplished that with low swoopy fenders, hideaway headlamps, and flush door handles.

This long history of giving the public glimpses of the future had a purpose beyond merely sparking the imagination of potential customers. These styling exercises would be used to test future directions in design, features, and function without making an expensive mistake in production.

In fact, one of the earliest examples of a futuristic car to go directly into production without the benefit of testing a concept first was the 1934 Chrysler Airflow. It was a marketing disaster on the same scale as the Edsel some 24 years later.

The Airflow was a sleek aerodynamic study inspired by a teardrop shape at a time when cars sported formal upright grilles and squared-off passenger cabins. And at a time when people actually believed in the concept of being thrown clear of a wreck, the Airflow boasted a steel safety cage beneath the skin for occupant protection. In addition to being launched during the depths of the Great Depression, the Airflow was deemed ugly by a buying public used to more conventional cars. As a result of its cool reception, Chrysler quickly restyled and renamed the car Airstream for the 1935 model year.

Chrysler's own history of concept cars didn't begin until 1941 when it built two "image cars," the Imperial LeBaron Newport and Thunderbolt. The Newport dual cowl phaeton featured hideaway headlamps and flowing fenders like the Y-Job. It was used to pace the Indy 500 and as a parade car. The two-seat Thunderbolt, created by Alex Tremulis, who later designed the Tucker, was a futuristic study that, in addition to having a power retractable hardtop,

Chrysler's Airflow, developed without the benefit of a show car to condition the public to its radical new styling, touted a swept-back aerodynamic look when most cars sported stand-up grilles and squared-off cabins. After disappointing sales, the more conventional-looking 1935 model was renamed Airstream. *Chrysler*

The 1941 Thunderbolt, above, was one of two "image cars" built by Chrysler. In addition to a retractable top, the Alex Tremulis design featured fenders incorporated in the body. Virgil Exner commissioned the Italian Ghia studio to do a series of show cars in the 1950s including the 1953 d'Elegance, below which later inspired the 1998 Chronos concept. *Chrysler*

fully integrated the fenders into the body, a major departure in auto design.

Show cars enjoyed a heyday in the 1950s. Design studios churned them out by the hundreds. General Motors stocked its traveling Motorama exhibits with dream machines named Buick Wildcat and Pontiac Banshee, along with exercises like the Chevy Corvette and Nomad, which would form the basis of production models. Ford dabbled with improbable ideas like the nuclear-powered Nucelon and the Lincoln Futura, which became better known after "Kustom King" George Barris got his hands on it and turned it into the Batmobile for 1960s television.

Chrysler's chief designer Virgil Exner commissioned a series of show cars from the Italian Ghia design studio throughout that era, from the aptly named d'Elegance (which would later inspire the 1998 Chrysler Chronos) to the Norseman, which had the dubious distinction of going down with the Andrea Doria in 1956.

The trend continued into the 1960s with some fairly significant studies, such as the 1963 Chrysler Turbine cars, Buick's Silver Arrow, which would become the Riviera, and the Corvette Manta Ray, which developed the shape for the 1968 Sting Ray.

Somewhere between the go-go 1960s and the resurgent 1980s, the flame of inspiration flickered and died. An industry that suddenly had to cope with safety, fuel economy, and emission issues didn't have time for dream cars. The realities of meeting higher corporate fuel economy standards and tighter emission regulations while figuring out air-bags and other safety features just didn't leave the resources or the desire to take these flights of fancy. The industry had to keep an eye on business, and business was pretty scary then, with two energy crises, a crush of new regulations to meet, crippling recessions, labor strife, and increasing competition from imports.

Dream cars just weren't the same. When they began to reappear in the 1980s, more often than not they were pure aerodynamic shapes that were merely test beds for exotic engine technology. Ford's Probe series was designed to test just how slippery a car could be in the race to reduce aerodynamic drag. Oldsmobile's Aerotech was designed to set a closed-circuit speed record, while Buick resurrected the Wildcat series to show off its prowess in building V-6 engines. Even Chevy's Corvette concept was more for show than a predictor of future design for the fifth generation Corvette.

Against this backdrop, Chrysler was quietly struggling after its highly publicized return to profitability from near certain bankruptcy in the early 1980s. By mid-decade, the cars that had saved the company's bacon had all the appeal of day-old doughnuts. It had ridden its mini-van and multitude of K-car derivatives just about as far as it could. The company was running out of steam just as tough economic times for the entire industry loomed on the horizon.

In design, Chrysler was purely reactive. It didn't lead, it followed. The undisputed king was Ford's Vice President of Design Jack Telnack. With the aerodynamic-inspired "jellybean" look of the 1983 Thunderbird and the 1986 Taurus, Ford was calling the shots at a time when General Motors was still stinging from criticism that all its cars were badge-engineered lookalikes.

Yet Chrysler knew it had to change in order to survive. After a long internal study, the management team of Iacocca, Lutz, Gale, Castaing, and purchasing chief Tom Stallkamp came to the conclusion that a new way of building cars, using platform teams, was necessary for survival. It was a revolutionary method of building cars by breaking down the walls that separated engineering, design, purchasing, and manufacturing. In its place was a leaner, faster company. But given the steady diet of lackluster cars

The first recognized concept car is Harley Earl's Buick Y-Job from 1938. The Y-Job's distinguishing characteristics include hideaway headlamps, no running boards, and a lower, wider, longer look that would define American auto design for generations to come. *Buick*

Concept cars enjoyed their first golden age throughout the 1950s and 1960s. The public had a chance to drive about 50 Ghia-bodied Chrysler Turbine cars in a program that eventually demonstrated that the jet engine was not suitable for use in automobiles. *Chrysler*

being served up, who would believe that a change of this magnitude was under way and that a new Chrysler Corporation was being born? And even though the new system could produce an all-new vehicle faster than the traditional six years, it would still be four years at best before the new products and this new way of doing business would be evident to both the public and Wall Street.

The challenge was to convince a skeptical world that Chrysler had a plan. "We had to do something about our credibility," Gale says. "We needed to have something to say about design, about the future. So we took a gamble."

That gamble was to revive the concept car, not as some far-out dream machine to entertain show goers, but

rather as a way of tipping off the press, Wall Street analysts, the banking community, and the public that there were some interesting products in Chrysler's future.

"We had a well-reasoned business motive for doing concept cars, but there was also the issue of personal pride involved," Lutz recalls. "Here we were, being beaten up in the press and justifiably so. So what do you do in the meantime when your bankers, the press, the analysts, and your dealers are asking 'Why don't you guys do this?' or 'Why don't you guys do that?' and 'Why don't you guys get it?' You can only say for so long, 'Look, we get it, trust us, we're going to do great cars. Yes, I know what you mean, I know we shouldn't do padded vinyl roofs anymore.' But

Even in 1963, concepts like the Buick Silver Arrow I were used to predict the shape of future production cars, in this case the 1964 Riviera. *Buick*

the only way you can really get them to shut up and demonstrate that, 'Look, we know what you're talking about and help is on the way,' is by doing concept cars.

"That's the quickest way to signal that yes, we understand," Lutz continues. "It's going to take awhile to get the production turned around, but we understand what we have been doing wrong, and what you see here is a demonstration of what we are going to do in the future.' That was our prime purpose. It gets to be a personal thing. You almost wind up doing the best work partly for yourself. So it was on Tom Gale's and my part, a very strong desire to personally prove, that we

too, the two of us, can do better than what you're seeing out there."

By doing Portofino, Millennium, and Viper, Chrysler added a new reason for doing concept cars: credibility. It wanted to say to the world, "This is what we're capable of. Watch us deliver."

In establishing this credibility, it was also the first step, albeit almost unknowingly, in a process that would use concept cars like the Portofino for strategic purposes in long-range product planning, something no other car company was doing. Viper, a marketing masterstroke, represented yet another facet to the concept car gambit. If

By the mid-1980s, concept cars no longer related to the cars that the public could buy. Instead they were sleek aerodynamic studies used to showcase technology. The 1985 Buick Wildcat was used to promote the division's V-6 engines. *Buick*

Portofino was a tentative step in a strategic, long-range product planning process, then Viper was a bold, tactical punch to give the company a lift when it needed it the most. The overwhelming reaction to the Viper concept car at the 1989 North American International Auto Show in Detroit galvanized the idea of taking a show car into production and using it as a marketing tool, morale booster, and a public rallying point for the underdog of the domestic industry.

"We respond to the enthusiast press," Gale admits. "You don't see us do a lot of black concept cars that they can't photograph. Instead you'll see reds and yellows. We

do things that we hope will get magazine covers. With the Viper, we got more third party endorsements and credible reporting that did more for our image than all the advertising we could ever do. It's worth its weight in gold. If we went out and had to buy all the exposure the Viper got, we couldn't do it—at least not for the relative pittance that the concept car cost us."

In fact, this equation is so persuasive that Gale has never been a big proponent of motorsports as a promotional tool. "You go through a lot of money fast in racing. I could do 10 years' worth of concept cars for one year of racing money."

What the concept cars did for Chrysler, externally, was buy time. They kept many eyes focused on the future rather than the rocky economic times the company was weathering.

Something else was also happening on the inside. Gale made it a practice for each studio to work on a concept car alongside regular production work. As the production models progressed, bits of the show cars in the same studio would rub off on them, including the names. "Many of the names of our cars came from the show cars, starting with Viper," Gale observes. Others included the Neon, Prowler, Cirrus, and Stratus.

And the shapes had an influence on production thinking. "There is a surface ethic, a surface continuity from these show cars that translates directly into the production models," Gale explains. "Look at some of the things we did in previewing the Ram truck with the LRT concept, as well as the design themes that have played out on the front of the 300M and LHS. Would we have done these things without the concept cars? I don't think so.

"As a result, concept cars, in our case, are much more meaningful," Gale explains. "It is evidence that concept cars really are part of the product development process. It also says that our concept cars are not artificial. Most of the time the things that really resonated with people were the things they could visualize as being real, like Viper and Prowler. Concepts have evolved to the point where we try to live up to a customer's expectation and not to a designer's expectation, nor a manufacturer's expectation. It has to be a plausible thing that we are doing."

The value of seemingly production-ready concept cars has made other car companies stand up and take notice. For instance, Ford has evolved from doing far-out dream machines like the V-12 Indigo to showcasing fairly faithful executions of future products, like the revived Thunderbird.

"We are now where concept cars can be quite literal, and we allow for some speculation as to whether or not we will actually do them," Gale says. He quickly adds with an

Before Chrysler developed the idea of doing concept cars that seriously foreshadowed production trends, it was prone to doing unrealistic one-off exercises like the Plymouth Speedster, a small open sports car that sought to offer the wind-in-your-face excitement of riding a motorcycle. *Chrysler*

impish grin, "In a way that creates some internal pressure to actually create them."

As a result, at Chrysler concept cars have become an integral link to developing new products. This approach encourages designers to use all the freedom that they've always enjoyed when drawing dream cars with the added incentive that their vehicle just might go into series production.

Between 1987 and 1999, Chrysler produced nearly 50 concept cars, of which more than a quarter have become vehicles the public could buy. In doing so, the company redefined for the auto industry the purpose and worth of doing dream cars for the public.

CHAPTER THREE

LH MEANS MORE THAN LAST HOPE

By 1990, Chrysler's sales were hitting bottom. Though the press and Wall Street analysts were impressed with the Viper, the company had done little to prove to the public that it had indeed turned a corner internally and was intent on radically changing not just the designs of the cars it sold, but also the way it made them.

According to Bob Lutz in his book *Guts: The Seven Laws of Business that Made Chrysler the World's Hottest Car Company*, the company turned a profit of only $68 million in 1990 and lost $795 million in 1991.

"But equally as troubling as our erosion in profitability," Lutz writes, "was the fact that our pension fund in 1991 was underfunded to the tune of $4.3 billion (the largest such deficit in all of American industry), our credit rating was shot (some of our debt was selling at junk bond levels), and our stock price had plummeted from its 1989 peak of just under $30 a share to just over $10."

Chrysler's product line-up was a mess too. The flagships of the Chrysler brand were K-car-derived New York-ers and Imperials, still boxy and decked with chrome and padded vinyl and fake wire wheel covers. Dodge had the Dynasty and the Monaco, a rebadged version of the Eagle Premier, which was, by way of the AMC acquisition, a re-engineered Renault 25. Chrysler performance, with heritage going back to the Mopar muscle car era, saw the torch being carried by the Dodge Daytona, Plymouth Laser, and Eagle Talon. The Daytona, also K-derived, tried to offer brutish power from turbocharged 2.2-liter four-cylinder engines. The Laser and Talon were merely versions of the Mitsubishi Eclipse, which were being built in Illinois at the Chrysler-Mitsubishi joint venture plant called Diamond-Star.

The midsize family segment was covered by the forgettable Dodge Spirit and Plymouth Acclaim, cars built off the new A-platform. They weren't exactly K-clones, but their conservative styling didn't set the world on fire, either. In the small car segment were the P-cars, the Dodge Shadow and Plymouth Sundance, which tried but

Neon displays a strong roof arch and cute, huggable looks, thanks to the round headlamps and soft hood contour. *Chrysler*

Eagle Optima, which debuted in 1990, accurately forecast the look of Chrysler's LH sedans, which would bow two years later. *John Lamm*

never could quite match the volumes of the cars they replaced, the Dodge Omni and Plymouth Horizon, successful knock-offs of the VW Golf. Then there was the odd assortment of Colts, subcompacts from Mitsubishi, sold under both Plymouth and Dodge brands and as Summits by Eagle.

The mainstay of the Chrysler franchise, the ground-breaking minivan, was still a year away from its first major redesign since its introduction as a 1984 model.

Chrysler's cupboard was bare when it came to new products. Against that backdrop, the joke circulating among Detroit industry insiders was that LH, the code name for Chrysler's make-or-break full-size family sedan, was Last Hope. The joke stung, but only because it contained more than a grain of truth.

Talking about a turnaround is one thing; seeing is believing. At the 1990 North American International Auto

Show, Chrysler took the wraps off the Eagle Optima, a vehicle that would figure prominently in the company's recovery.

The shape of the Optima, with its cab forward architecture, was sleek, aerodynamic, and far more advanced than any of the boxy production cars that populated Chrysler's stand. Though the rear-drive Optima was powered by a 4.0-liter 32-valve V-8 that would never see production, the north-south arrangement was similar to the way the new family of V-6 engines would be mounted. The LH would be front drive, but the Optima's layout was part of the management team's hope to someday field a rear-drive luxury based off this new platform.

Two versions of the Optima were actually developed—one with a transverse engine layout, the other with the longitudinal mount. While both rode on essentially the same platform, the look was totally different. The longitudinal-engined car was more aggressive in its cab forward appearance.

"We were trying to figure out a way to package the front and really push the front-door proportion and balance up the front and rear doors," Gale says. "Up until then, you were really taking the space away from the rear doors into the front doors and into the trunk. One is basically where GM is today with its sedans and the other is what we did. That's what gave us the windshield so far out over the dash. When you look at the shape of the windshield and the centerline of the cars, there is a dramatic difference."

The Optima's sleek cab forward shape gave it a sporty feel while retaining the functionality of a four-door family sedan. The Optima rode on a 112-inch wheelbase and had an overall length of 193.7 inches. It stood 55 inches tall and 74.6 inches wide and had 17-inch body-colored wheels shod with Goodyear Eagle P245/50ZR-17 tires. The car was painted in a three-coat pearlescent white, while the interior was finished in a quartz gray with blue accents.

At the same time the Optima was unveiled, the Dodge LRT concept, which was also destined for the show circuit, was previewed for the press, but then at the last minute yanked from the public display. Lee Iacocca feared that too much exposure would tip the competition on Dodge's bold new truck styling theme. Gale says the show property was eventually destroyed.

The LRT (which stood for Little Red Truck) had aggressive fenders and stand up hood, projecting the attitude of a big rig. Though it accurately predicted the look of the Ram, it was actually based on the smaller Dakota platform to throw off the competition when they poked around the vehicle taking measurements. Even this bit of gamesmanship wouldn't prove enough. Iacocca's fears were confirmed when pictures of the LRT circulated and Ford responded at the 1995 auto show with a macho show truck of its own called the Triton, which foretold the bold styling on its heavy-duty pickup line.

Optima's 4.0-liter V-8 and rear-drive layout would never see production. Still, the longitudinal orientation of the powertrain was consistent with the front-drive V-6 production models. *John Lamm*

The LRT was an interesting study nonetheless. Power came from an unspecified V-8 engine (more gamesmanship) that had multipoint fuel injection and a unique "beer keg" intake manifold cast in aluminum. The new manifold was designed to test the optimal intake runner length, yet was compact enough to help lower the hood line.

The LRT was a convertible with retractable metal panels that stowed behind the bucket seats. The electronically operated top mechanism moved these panels up and down through a track mounted in the sport bar. Two off-road lighting units on the top of the bar automatically flipped up to allow the top to be opened or closed.

At the rear of the truck, vinyl webbing replaced the traditional tailgate and could be automatically retracted

Hoping to misdirect the competition, the LRT, shown here at the pre-show press preview, is built to midsize Dodge Dakota dimensions. However, Lee Iacocca felt too much exposure would tip the company's hand. The truck never made it to an auto show and was eventually destroyed. *John Lamm*

into the floor to provide access to the load space. And instead of conventionally mounting the taillamps into the end of the box, they were contained in the rear bumper surface. Three-spoke 17-inch wheels and tires similar to the Viper's were also used on the LRT.

The LRT demonstrated that Chrysler was not afraid to use design to polarize potential customers. You either loved or hated the "in your face" look of the LRT and the production Ram that would follow. Considering that Chrysler had less than 5 percent of the full-size pickup market, it was a gamble that would pay off. Enough people liked the radical new look that the company's market penetration actually climbed to nearly 20 percent.

"We knew there was going to be a visual shock with the Ram pickup," Lutz says, "so we wanted to blunt it a little bit by doing the show vehicle first. But we also shortened the competitor's reaction time. When we showed the Dodge LRT [to the press], we sent Ford scrambling back to the drawing board to redo what they started doing. You always run the risk of doing that, especially if people take you seriously and see that what you are doing in concept vehicles is going to translate into reality."

The LRT is but one example of Chrysler's struggle to figure out the best way to use show cars. Viper and Optima were confidence builders, but LRT gave pause to the argument that perhaps the company risked giving away the store on future product plans. It was clear that Chrysler hadn't fully integrated the idea of doing concept cars into the product development process, as evidenced by the Neon.

The Neon show car, which bowed in 1991, was a cute, huggable subcompact that picked up in styling where the original Beetle left off. With its round headlights and strong roof arch (again reinforcing the cab forward look that Chrysler pioneered), the Neon projected a fun image. It featured a retractable canvas roof and fully reclining removable seats, which were simple aluminum frames covered with detachable foam cushions. The Neon had sliding front and rear doors that opened to a B-pillarless cabin, which eased entry and exit as well as a trunk that could be opened conventionally or slid out like a drawer.

A small research group called the Alternative Engine Taskforce, which reported to engineering chief Francois Castaing, developed the Neon's unconventional two-stroke powerplant. It used External Breathing Direction Injection (EBDI) technology, which replaced the traditional valve-train with simple open ports that were opened and closed by movement of the piston. As a result, the 1.1-liter engine had half the components used to assemble a conventional engine and weighed 40 percent less. Yet the little engine was capable of producing over 100 horsepower.

Castaing says the AET group built a whole series of two-stroke engines, but the project was later abandoned due to accelerating development costs at a time when four-stroke technology was meeting all the company's fuel economy and emission objectives.

The Neon concept also touted a high level of recyclable parts. Interior panels were labeled to identify the type of plastic, further easing the process. Other Neon features included aluminum wheels made from recycled material fitted with large diameter, low rolling resistance P175/65R-17 tires, specially coated glass designed to absorb ultraviolet light, the use of water-borne paint, and even a manual on-board trash compactor!

The show car's dimensions were similar to the production car—both shared a 104-inch wheelbase, while the 66.5-inch width was only 1 inch narrower than the "real"

Work on the Neon show car actually started after the more conservatively styled production model was nearly finished. These sketches show the roll-back canvas roof and the unique sliding side doors. *Chrysler*

Neon. Overall length was 4 inches shorter at 167.7, and with its strongly arched roof, the concept car was 5 inches taller, at 57.2 inches.

"The Neon was an exercise in reinventing the small car," Lutz explains. "You're never going to solve the small car profitability dilemma if you think of small cars merely as scaled-down versions of big cars. It's only when you completely realign your thinking, think out of the box, and look at an entirely different way of executing a small car, that you're going to break through the cost paradigm. The car that always stood out as a benchmark as completely revising your thinking is the Citroen 2CV. The original Neon concept had a lot of Citroen 2CV thinking in it: thin seats with pads over thin tubes, large canvas sunroof."

Neon's seats were simply constructed of aluminum tubing with detachable cushions suspended from them. The seats could be removed and used as beach chairs. *John Lamm*

But the likeable concept car bore little resemblance to the design intended for production. The production Neon, which was already in the works when the show car was being designed, was conceived as a sedan, coupe, and even convertible. Though slightly rounded, Neon still looked too much like Chrysler's existing line-up. The grille was flanked with cat-eye-shaped headlamps, not the round bug eyes of the show car. In fact, the nose, thanks to the boxy shape, looked a lot like the front end of the minivans.

"My one regret is we didn't have the guts to execute the real Neon more closely to what the concept car looked like," Lutz says. "We sort of let ourselves be conventionalized." Lutz concedes things like the pillarless cabin design were not feasible, but he believes the production car could have been much closer in shape and execution.

"In the production process, as a result of the marketing guys, we went away from the round headlights and went to the cat-eye headlamps," Lutz adds. "It was relatively late in the program when one of our bankers, Dick Bott from Credit Suisse, and several other people told us it was a nice little car, but that we totally lost any of the uniqueness and personality of the concept car. We looked at it, doubled back and went back to the concept car headlights and adopted as many features as we could, including the wheel covers. The Neon did well, but I think it would have done even better had it stayed closer to the concept."

One vehicle that didn't stay close to the concept was the major overhaul of the minivan in 1996. The 1992 EPIC minivan was a calculated move to throw the competition off on design themes for the vehicle's replacement. Boxy, with upright sides and very little body development, the EPIC looked newer than the existing minivan but lacked the flared wheel arches and expansive glass area of the new van.

The EPIC did have a nicely rounded back end and curved D-pillar that was not dissimilar to the redesigned van, but the front end was blunter, with no break between the hood and the windshield. That look, according to Lutz, was closer to the second generation Renault Espace.

Chrysler's press materials were pushing the fact that this design was influenced by cab forward. The press kit stated that the "cab forward look gives the minivan a very aggressive appearance. The windshield, although aggressively raked, blends with the overall design because of a unique approach to the A-pillar that doesn't exaggerate the distance from the door to the cowl of the hood."

This was a direct shot at General Motors' APV minivans, the so-called "dustbusters" that had elongated hoods and steeply raked windshields. In fact, at the same show, GM showed a concept van, the Sizigi, that showcased a much shorter snout that would later be incorporated in the APV. Except for the curved back end on the EPIC, both vans were remarkably alike in appearance.

Still, EPIC did predict many customer-friendly details that would be used on the 1996 redesign of the minivan,

RENKERT

EPIC was intended to show that a major redesign on Chrysler's minivan was in the works, without giving away solid clues as to what it would look like. *Chrysler*

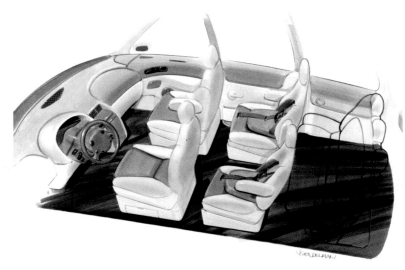

Interior sketches show some features that would go into production, like integrated child safety seats and a third-row seat that folds into the floor. While Chrysler never fully developed the "stow and go" third seat, Honda introduced it on its Odyssey minivan. *Chrysler*

In profile, the EPIC has a clean, modern shape with a steeply raked hood and windshield. Chrysler's next generation minivan, however, would sport fender flares, a larger glass area, and a distinct break between the hood and windshield. *John Lamm*

principally the left-hand sliding door. It was also Chrysler's first experiment with child safety seats integrated into the rear captain's chairs. And while it took Honda to bring the idea to the market first with the Odyssey minivan, EPIC had a third seat, called "stow and go" that folded flat into the floor. ("Honda measured the heck out of that," Gale says, adding, "We know of one company, a domestic competitor, that actually got into the show after hours and templated a few of our concepts.")

EPIC also experimented with a small steering wheel, almost like that on a racecar, which allowed the driver to look over, rather than through, the wheel to see the instrument panel.

Above all, EPIC was a technical exercise for the Liberty group, a small, advanced product team that was originally charged with building a new small car for Chrysler (see Chapter 7).

EPIC's acronym stood for Electric Power Inter-urban Commuter. Using nickel-iron batteries, Chrysler projected a range of 120 miles and a top speed of 65 miles per hour. A 54-kilowatt DC motor provided the power, which was transmitted through a two-speed automatic transmission. EPIC was equipped with an automatic watering system for the batteries, which was said to minimize maintenance.

Chrysler believed that vans provided the best possible platform for electric vehicle development because of the flat floor, which allows for better packaging of the battery pack. In fact, the battery pack and electric drive system for EPIC was adapted from Chrysler's full-size B-van experimental vehicle called the TEVan.

EPIC's proportions were close to the 1996 redesigned van. Both shared a 119.3-inch wheelbase and were just under 68 inches tall. EPIC was 1/2-inch wider at 77.4 inches, but 9.6 inches shorter in overall length at 190.1. Unlike the production van, EPIC was equipped with huge wheels and tires, P195/55R-19s in the front and P195/55R-20s in the rear.

If Chrysler wasn't about to give away the store with the looks of the EPIC, it was hoping to convert some skeptics of its plan to radically revamp the Spirit/Acclaim compacts. The Chrysler Cirrus, which also debuted in 1992, was a pure styling exercise that, while not accurately showing what the company's new JA cars (Cirrus/Stratus) would look like, hinted that cab forward could be taken to a level beyond the LH.

"It was another Pacifica car," Gale says. "It was very much in the spirit of the Portofino." The Cirrus was another design with no B-pillar and doors that opened suicide fashion. The wheels were squarely at the corners and there was little or no break from the hoodline to the windshield, giving the Cirrus almost a monospace or one-box look. The Cirrus was fairly compact with an overall length of only 187 inches. It seated four passengers comfortably in individual buckets separated by front and rear consoles.

Cirrus also sported a wooden buck of a proposed two-stroke engine from the AET, the same group that provided the Neon concept car powerplant. Only this engine, a supercharged V-6 called "Fury," was envisioned to produce a whopping 400 horsepower.

Still, Cirrus didn't generate the same sort of buzz, Gale believes, because it wasn't a runner. "This was still while we hadn't quite developed our process for concept cars," Gale explains. "This was before we realized the tremendous payback from just making them run. Cirrus did give us the name for the car and some of the graphics. In retrospect, I wish the JAs (Cirrus and Stratus) reached as far as the concept."

Even though it didn't run, the Cirrus demonstrated that cab forward was the company's design signature, and all the talk of 400 horsepower engines meant high performance was still alive and kicking at Chrysler.

Cirrus further explores cab forward architecture, this time on Chrysler's midsize JA platform. Although the production Cirrus took its name from the show car, its shape was not this extreme. *Chrysler*

Like the front, the rear taillamp theme was not adapted for Cirrus production. *John Lamm*

The two-stroke V-6 engine that promised 400 horsepower is merely a wood mock-up in the Cirrus show car. *John Lamm*

ANSWERING QUESTIONS NO ONE ASKED

At the 1990 North American International Auto Show, as Tom Gale stood near the Chrysler Voyager III concept vehicle, Chuck Jordan, then GM's design chief, reportedly walked over and said, "So, Lutz finally got someone to build it for him."

"It" was a two-piece vehicle with a small, three-passenger urban commuter up front and a detachable back half that could increase total vehicle capacity to eight people.

"I was trying to push that idea in automobile company after automobile company after automobile company," Bob Lutz freely admits, having tried it on the design staffs at BMW, Opel, GM, Ford, and finally Chrysler. "I've always been intrigued by this concept of the freeway cruiser and urban module. Sooner or later it will come to that. The inner city areas will become so crowded that the word is going to be vehicles under two meters in length only will be allowed.

"At home I've got a zillion sketches. I tried to get Chuck Jordan to do one like that at Opel, and at BMW I thought what if we do two motorscooters that will dock into the sides of the vehicle?" Lutz says. "I just couldn't get anyone to do it."

He adds that part of the inspiration for Voyager III comes from the James Bond movie *Thunderball*, where Largo's yacht separates and the large rear end wallows in the water while the smaller front end takes off.

Lutz discussed the project with Neil Walling, who was head of advanced design. Lutz adds that Voyager III "was done purely for fun, with no production in mind, just to have an extreme, attention-getting display."

When docked together, the two modules had a wheelbase of 122 inches and the overall length was 198.5 inches, shorter than the company's LH sedans. The front module's rear wheels were retracted once the vehicle was joined, while tandem rear axles with four wheels supported the rear.

A clean-burning propane-fueled 1.6-liter four-cylinder engine powered the front urban commuter, while the 2.2-liter gasoline engine drove the rear wheels. When combined,

Chrysler Bob Lutz's pet project, the Voyager III vehicle-within-a-vehicle, finally gets built. The propane-powered, three-passenger "command module" is detached from Voyager III and is ready for urban commuting. *Chrysler*

Despite its compact appearance, the front-drive Aviat holds four passengers with a rear seat about the same size as a LeBaron convertible. *John Lamm*

the concept called for the front engine to do all the work, with the electronically coupled rear engine kicking in only when extra power was needed for acceleration.

"It was a concept car that only those crazy guys at Chrysler would do," Lutz says. "It was interesting in that you could actually demonstrate it docking and undocking."

Whimsy is the order of the day on this Neon-based exercise called Expresso. *Chrysler*

Ease of exit and entry is an Expresso hallmark. It is designed to be a taxicab of the future. *Chrysler*

Runners-up to the Voyager III in wackiness were the Neon Aviat and the Expresso, which were unveiled in 1994.

Described as a sport coupe for the 21st century, the Aviat was an extreme aerodynamic study built with Neon components. It resembled a teardrop-shaped bicycle helmet with the rear wheels set on wings that separated them from the tapered back end. The rear suspension was unique: lower tri-links and modified upper A-arm, which attached the wheel in the outrigger.

According to Lutz, the brief for Aviat was to find a way "to do a highly aerodynamic, exciting, Jaray-type coupe with an extreme shape and pick up some of those channeled air concepts from the Bertone B.A.T."

While a transversely mounted 145-horsepower 2.0-liter four-cylinder engine drove the Aviat's front wheels, the radiators were located in the rear to help improve airflow. Aerodynamic tests of a three-eighths scale model of the Aviat showed a drag coefficient of 0.20, the best of any Chrysler vehicle and close to that of an F-16 jet fighter, which is 0.16.

Even though the tapered Aviat looked small—it was only 168.8 inches long but rode on a 108.5-inch wheelbase—it had room for four inside. In fact, Chrysler boasted that the rear seat was about the same width as the LeBaron convertible's.

A unique feature on the interior was an instrument cluster and control panel that moved with the steering wheel to keep them in view of, and easily accessible to, the driver at all times.

While the Aviat had a practical aerodynamic application for its unusually styled body, the Expresso was pure whimsy. Designed as a sort of futuristic taxicab, the sides of the Expresso, with its hooded side glass and sash-mounted door handles, looked like a set of eyes.

Based on a shortened Neon platform and powered by the same 132-horsepower 2.0-liter four-cylinder engine, the Expresso was meant to draw attention to the production car's fun-to-drive character. Though it had only a 91-inch wheelbase and was a compact 141.6 inches in overall length, the Expresso was, at 69.1 inches, 15 inches taller than the Neon.

"In a goofy way, the Expresso was a precursor to the tall roof PT Cruiser," Gale says. The taller roof meant the seating could be upright, which allowed the storage under the front buckets to match the underseat space of an airline seat. And the passenger-side bucket could be folded forward for additional cargo carrying capacity, another feature found on the 2001 PT Cruiser.

The ease of bag handling was one of the major criteria driving the Expresso's unorthodox shape. "When people travel, they pack for a certain mode of transportation," said Walling at Expresso's launch. "One of the approaches to the interior design of Expresso was to look at the often harried transition from an airplane to a taxi. When you get off an airplane, you have to stuff all your baggage in the trunk of a vehicle that doesn't have any relationship to the one that you just left. It's interesting to us when you design something for specific use, frequently you find that the family usage is also enhanced. Expresso is simply a more sensible taxi that is also great for families and commuters."

The Expresso also predicted several technologies that would become commonplace on cars by the end of the decade. It had an onboard navigation system as well as a rear seat entertainment system that would allow the passengers to watch a movie or play video games.

The Plymouth Backpack was another attempt at finding a niche where none existed. This 1995 concept combined a small cabin with a tiny pickup bed. Walling called it a "crossover vehicle for young, active people who want to go everywhere, do everything, and have a great time doing it."

The proportions of the Backpack were radically different for such a small vehicle. It was tall—65.1 inches relative to its short 91.7-inch wheelbase and 142-inch overall length. Though 20 inches shorter than Neon, it had minivan-like stature, which provided an upright seating position for its passengers. And its 72-inch width gave enough space for the driver's seat to move a quarter turn inward and use the flat folding passenger seat as a workspace.

The small pickup bed could be fitted with racks to carry everything from mountain bikes to scuba gear, and there was additional, lockable storage beneath the floor of the box. In addition to accommodating two up front, a small retractable center-mounted jump seat in the back provided space to carry an additional passenger.

Backpack explores the tall-car theme with a twist—it's a small pickup and an urban commuter. *Chrysler, John Lamm*

A 2.0-liter four-cylinder engine from the Neon propels the Backpack down the road with 135 horsepower. *John Lamm*

The mechanicals of Backpack came from the Neon. It was powered by a 135-horsepower 2.0-liter four-cylinder engine and was equipped with a three-speed automatic transmission. Though Backpack didn't make it into production, it foreshadowed the current trend to equip SUVs with small pickup beds as well as the shift to "tall-car" proportions that raise the roof to provide more chair-like seating positions.

CHAPTER FOUR

PERFORMANCE RULES

The Viper's unqualified success in generating positive press for Chrysler opened the lid on the toy box for the car guys in upper management. Freed of the old "bean counter" paradigm that each product line had to have significant volume and be profitable in order to merit consideration, Chrysler plunged forward with the kinds of cars that few would actually buy but many would want to read about or see in the flesh.

Two examples were Lutz's coupe version of the Viper, called the GTS, followed in short order by Tom Gale's pet project, the Prowler: a modern, factory-built two-seater that would pay tribute to America's hot rod culture.

No doubt, the Viper RT/10 roadster was a hit. The initial 200 built for the 1992 model year instantly became prized collectibles. The 1993 production run of some 2,000 cars quickly sold out and a huge order bank developed. Still, the car lacked the kind of refinement that would allow someone to drive it most of the year. But more important, the Viper needed a new shape if it was going to be successful in racing.

As early as 1992, work began on the coupe version with clay models mocked up over the RT/10's side pipes and three-spoke wheels. The original GTS drawings show a dual rear exhaust and the capped exposed side pipes. Later the idea was to keep the same routing of the pipes through the sills but encase them within the rocker panels. One of the chief complaints of the Viper Roadster was that you heard only one bank of the V-10 engine. The dual rear exhaust gave off the full measure of the V-10's sound and was later adapted to the roadster.

In doing the coupe, Gale had wanted a look not dissimilar to the Ferrari 250 GTO or the legendary Cobra Daytona Coupe, penned by Shelby designer Peter Brock. In fact, Brock told Matt Stone in his book *Viper* that "Tom Gale came to me with some of the original drawings of the GTS Coupe in the previous August [1992] at the Pebble Beach Concours d'Elegance and asked my opinion of the new car. He wanted to make sure that I had no problem with the resemblance to the Daytona, especially the blue

In addition to a NACA air inlet, the front of the GTS has a large, aerodynamic splitter accentuated by the bold striping. *John Lamm*

GTS's interior reflects the efforts to convert the Viper from a weekend toy to a serious, year-round performance car. *Chrysler*

and white paint scheme. I was flattered that they would even consider asking my permission."

In addition to the roof, the GTS Coupe incorporated a hatchback rear window, power door glass, contoured roof blisters to increase headroom, an NACA duct on the hood to improve engine breathing, and a chromed fuel filler door styled to resemble a quick release racing fuel cap. These refinements stood in stark contrast to the RT/10 Roadster, which had side curtains and a small fabric top, derisively called a toupee, which was assembled about as easily as a tent.

Some of the improvements on GTS Coupe were later applied to the Roadster, which ceased production for a year while the doors were converted from

Along with the launch of the GTS show car, the Ram VTS, done up in Viper's colors, introduced the cast iron V-10 to the full-size pickup line. *John Lamm*

side curtains to conventional glass and a new top was engineered.

The GTS Coupe was first shown at the 1993 Los Angeles Auto Show (along with the Ram VTS pickup that showcased the long awaited V-10 in Dodge's full-size truck) but wouldn't be launched until 1996. For that intro, Chrysler decided it would again play its European card. In introducing the production GTS Coupe for the 1996

model year at the Pebble Beach Concours d'Elegance in August of 1995, Lutz also took the wraps off the GTS-R racing version to compete at Le Mans as well as a Viper GTS pace car for the 1996 Indianapolis 500.

It should be noted that 1992 was a difficult year for Lutz. Even though the Viper had made it into production, on March 16 he was passed over for the top job at Chrysler, when Iacocca introduced Bob Eaton, who was

Bob Lutz wanted Viper to compete at Le Mans and commissioned the GTS-R racing version of the GTS. *Chrysler*

then chairman of GM Europe, as his hand-picked successor. Rumors ran wild that Lutz would bolt, most likely for a European manufacturer. The rumors were wrong. Lutz, who was always viewed as a strong-willed individual, proved to be the ultimate team player. And to his credit, Eaton, himself an engineer and enthusiast, let the team continue its work with minimal interference. Instead, the new chairman kept the business side humming and provided the crucial leadership to fend off a hostile takeover in 1996 by former chairman Iacocca and Chrysler shareholder Kirk Kerkorian.

While Lutz was setting his sights on Le Mans (and would later be responsible for the first factory-produced American car to win an FIA GT championship as well as class victories at the Sarthe circuit), Tom Gale was working with his designers to make a factory-produced hot rod.

Prowler sprang from an idea fair at Pacifica in 1991. "Anything was fair game," Gale says. "Anyone from the top designers to the guy who swept the floors could build a model. We had turtle cars and shark cars, all these outrageous little models and dioramas to help display them. In there was a hot rod and I was always into hot rods. We plucked it out and went into scale and eventually full size."

But the design didn't click. The young stylists who had worked on the car had developed a contemporary look with little or no retro cues. "It wasn't working from a form point of view," Gale says. "I came out for a review and told them I watched all this and if it didn't change, we'd pull it back to Auburn Hills."

Gale recommended that they visit some hot rod shows to get a real flavor for what the car should be. "Hot rodders go through phases for sure, but they're very traditional," Gale explains. "The cars are very honest to pure 1930s forms. Prowler needed to get back to that to make the imagery strong."

Eventually the designers got there. When the car was revealed the look was radical and the hot rod influence was obvious. "When we pulled the covers off, it

was magic," Gale says. "The show car was really sweet, compared even to the final product. Not to pick on ourselves, the wheel placement was much better, it wasn't as wide (as the production car). It was more what I wanted. But then, you didn't have to worry about side or front impacts with the show car. When you do what factories do to build a car, it's a wonder that the [production] car is as close as it is."

The Plymouth Prowler show car that was unveiled at the North American International Auto Show in 1993 featured an aluminum body and a 240-horsepower 3.5-liter V-6 engine driving the rear wheels through a four-speed sequential-shift automatic transaxle. The Prowler had a long 111.5-inch wheelbase to relatively short 161.1 overall length. The front 17-inch wheels had small cycle fenders covering them, while massive 20-inch wheels and tires were nestled under the rear fenders.

An early sketch shows the Prowler as a hot rod in concept, but with no retro cues. Gale ordered the designers to go back to the drawing board. *Chrysler*

There's no mistaking the hot rod heritage cue in the Prowler show car. *Chrysler*

The cycle fenders, small front bumpers, correct positioning of turn signals and brake lamps, and the inclusion of a high-mounted stoplight were designed to show that the Prowler could be built as a street legal machine, right down to the dual air bags.

There are a couple of features from the concept that didn't make it into production, like the electrically powered hardtop (production models have a manual soft top). Also note that the headlamps, which were flush on the concept car, are housed in blisters on the production models.

The first Prowlers were powered by a 214-horsepower 3.3-liter V-6; the larger 3.5-liter V-6 making 253 horsepower wasn't added until later. Still, the fact that a show car as wild as this could make it into production proved that the car-guy culture within Chrysler was thriving. Even more remarkable was that the company could make a low-volume roadster like the Prowler with an aluminum intensive body and price it at $40,000. The secret was the heavy reliance on off-the-shelf components, including an engine and transaxle originally designed for front-wheel-drive cars.

It was that flexibility and leanness in the system (the Prowler was actually done by the minivan group) that began attracting the notice of Wall Street and other manufacturers. It was also the reason Chrysler had returned to profitability by 1993 and was stockpiling money for the next downturn.

While Lutz had his Viper and Gale his Prowler, there was a third car-guy constituency within Chrysler that desperately wanted to revive the muscle car. This isn't to say that Gale, who in addition to building his own hot rod, wasn't a fan of muscle cars. One of his prized possessions is an AAR 'Cuda that he restored. But there were others like John Herlitz and Neil Walling, who cut their teeth as young designers on the original muscle cars, and they championed the idea of doing a modern asphalt-burner.

In 1994, they got their chance. In order to support the launch of the production Neon, all the show cars were ostensibly to be built off the new subcompact's floorpan. The three concepts were Venom, Aviat, and Expresso.

The production Prowler, shown here as the special Woodward Avenue edition, is wider than the show car. Also note the blistered headlamp treatment as opposed to the concept's flush lighting. *Chrysler*

Though the Venom used Neon's platform and instrument panel, the similarities end there. The rear-drive Venom borrowed suspension components and rear differential from the Viper. But instead of a V-10, the Venom used the corporate 3.5-liter V-6 from the LH tweaked to produce 245 horsepower and mated to a six-speed manual transmission. The Venom rode on a 106-inch wheelbase and was 182.6 inches in overall length, and stood 51.5 inches tall and 74.9 inches wide. Internally, the Venom signaled a real desire to do a rear-drive platform with the company's V-6 engines. And the styling seemed to say, "Let's stop borrowing other people's heritage (Cobra for Viper, 1932 Ford for Prowler) and use our own."

While the front of the Venom showed the influences of the Viper and Intrepid headlight and grille themes, the squared-off blunt nose also recalled the Coronet, while the blacked-out hood and tail end treatment echoed the Challenger and Barracuda. The side scoops were clearly influenced by the 1969 Dodge Charger. Even the paint, called "Venom yellow green pearl" was a tribute to the wild paint schemes of the 1960s.

Inside, the only cues that tied to the exterior were the "yellow green pearl" colored accents on the steering wheel, shift knob, and brake handle. The rest of the interior was done up in basic black with bolstered, leather-clad sport seats. Though the concept was rendered in metal, its design brief called for use of an aluminum body to minimize weight.

Unlike the cab rearward styling of the Challenger/Barracuda, the Venom's passenger compartment sat squarely in the middle of the car, with a steeply raked front windshield. Still, the body swept upward, imparting the same high belt feel of those original muscle cars.

But with both Viper GTS and Prowler in development, it didn't appear that the Venom was going to come out of the box. And unlike the Prowler, which was basically using front-drive components in a rear-drive layout, Chrysler still didn't believe that it could produce enough cars to justify the investment in a new rear-drive platform.

"I personally believe that we as a company will do a vehicle someday that represents what the Venom can do," Gale says, speaking of the car's muscle car retro styling, but more importantly of its rear-drive layout. "You'll notice that a pattern develops with things we've done over the years and they describe a proportion or a direction we're heading."

With Venom a no-go, the next attempt at finding a new definition of performance for Dodge fell to the Copperhead. This 1997 concept car was envisioned as an entry-level sports car that would provide a logical stepping stone to the Viper.

"If Dodge Viper is credited for reinventing the Shelby Cobra, then Dodge Copperhead should be credited for reinventing a car in the tradition of the Austin-Healey 3000," says John Herlitz.

Painted fire orange metallic, the Copperhead, at 72 inches wide and 167 inches long, was 3 inches narrower and 8 inches shorter than Viper. And yet, its wheels were

Prowler's interior carries the body color theme into the cockpit. Instruments are mounted in the center of the dash, except for the steering column-mounted tach, a tribute to hot rodders everywhere. *John Lamm*

pushed all the way out to the corners, giving it a wheelbase that, at 110 inches, was a foot longer.

The proportions were actually closer to that of the Plymouth Prowler, right down to the 20-inch rear wheels. This similarity in size gave rise to false expectations that the car could be easily built using the Plymouth's components right alongside the Viper at Chrysler's Conner Avenue assembly plant. In truth, the Copperhead's steel unit body and underpinnings were far different from the aluminum tub used to build Prowler.

But the Copperhead was a significant and interesting design study. Neil Walling says the Prowler-like proportions were intentional. "We designed Copperhead to look fast by utilizing minimal overhang and pushing the wheels way out to the front and rear corners."

Though the Copperhead sported Dodge's signature split grille, the fenders projected pontoon-like beyond the front fascia. The side detailing gave the car a lithe, athletic feel, thanks to an air extractor positioned just behind the front wheel that gave both the fender and the bodyside muscular curves. The rear end treatment was clean with large, jeweled taillamps and a single fin that bisected the trunk and was punctuated by the high-mounted stoplight. The fin was actually seven inches higher and was gradually whittled down to its finished height. The fin treatment picked up below the license plate frame and continued underneath the car. Chrome plated exhaust tips flanked the rear end.

The interior featured a unique dash layout. The only instrument in front of the driver was the tachometer; the rest of the analog gauges, including speedometer, were center mounted in a round opening that was intended to mimic a copperhead ready to strike. Beneath the instruments was a brushed aluminum pod with the radio and climate controls. The five-speed gated shifter sat atop a small center console. The seats were done up in a purple leather with a snakeskin pattern.

The Copperhead was powered by a 2.7-liter V-6 tuned to produce 220 horsepower. It was a preview of the

Venom recaptures the magic of the muscle car era. *John Lamm*

new base engine on the second-generation LH sedans.

At an estimated base price of $30,000, the Copperhead received a warm welcome. "Dodge dealers were frothing for it," Gale recalls. "But it was too close to Prowler in positioning and we already had Viper. I just didn't think that inasmuch as we could have used it in the marketplace, we just wouldn't haven't gotten as big a bang for the buck as we did with the other two. I would rather have something out there that would do more for us."

That more could have been the Plymouth Pronto Spyder, which was shown in 1998. Positioned with a base price of $20,000, the Pronto Spyder would have given Chrysler a line-up of sports cars that would make Hal Sperlich, who dreamed of Big Shot, Hot Shot, and Sling Shot, proud.

"I wanted Pronto Spyder," Lutz says. "Here is everyone doing two-passenger sports cars. BMW has the Z3, Mercedes has the SLK, Porsche has the Boxster, Mazda's got the Miata, and Honda's working on the S2000. Everybody, except Mazda, is in the $28,000 to $45,000 range and they're all going to have a big collision at the intersection because over time there won't be customers for all those cars. But what the world is really waiting for is the modern equivalent of the MGTC or the modern

Instead of a hairy V-8, Venom uses a V-6 engine to drive the rear wheels. *John Lamm*

equivalent of the Austin-Healey Sprite—a small, light-weight production sports car that has all the visual appeal of something like the Porsche Boxster. But you use high-volume, low-cost mechanical stuff, like a Neon twin-cam engine. You know 155 horsepower is going to be enough for that thing if we keep it light enough and simple enough. Offer it with one interior, one gearbox, one top, fabric, keep it simple and cheap, and go for a base price of $16,000, $17,000 or $18,000, but stay under $20,000 and you can sell a million of them."

There's more to keeping the price down besides using Neon components in the Pronto Spyder. It was proposed that the car use unpainted, recycled plastic, as demonstrated by two other concept cars, the CCV and the Pronto, to lower production costs.

"It could be made from the same material used to make plastic drinking bottles—polyethylene terephthalate

(PET)," says Tom Tremont, chief designer at the Pacifica studio where the Spyder was developed. "PET technology has the potential to reduce manufacturing costs by 80 percent over conventional methods of using steel."

While most automotive composites were costing between $5 and $10 per pound, recycled PET plastic was priced at only $1.50 a pound, a significant savings that could be used to lower the base price if it were to go into production.

But true to the dictum that all Chrysler concept cars are made out of metal, the Pronto Spyder was hand formed at Metalcrafters and painted with a matte finish to simulate the bonded-in color of a PET plastic body.

Plastic has other benefits as well. "The injection mold process allows us to do razor-sharp edges, precise intersections, and incised names and details," Tremont explains. "These forms are pure, precise, simple, and honest."

The Pronto Spyder was simply stunning. "We toyed around with naming it Gator because it looked like an alligator ready to strike its prey," says Tremont. "This car has a kinetic energy. The body central is slung down low between the wheels, suggesting a very low center of gravity."

In addition to the highly detailed, jeweled look of the front headlights, the taillamps and high-mounted stoplight on the Spyder were lit with neon tubes to provide more even illumination.

The Pronto Spyder had compact dimensions: a wheelbase of 95 inches and overall length of 156 inches. It was only 69 inches wide and 45 inches tall with the manually operated soft-top up. Power came from a 2.0-liter Neon four-cylinder engine bored out to 2.4-liters and supercharged to produce 225 horsepower. The front and rear MacPherson strut independent suspension was from the Neon parts bin.

While the exterior had a sharp-edged, machined look, Tremont says he "blended romantic detailing in the interior that hints at an earlier classic sports racer era." The five-speed manual gearbox (taken from the Neon

Copperhead is envisioned as an entry-level sports car for Dodge. *John Lamm*

ACR club racing package) had a chromed and gated shifter with a tortoise-shell finish knob that matched the steering wheel rim. The steering wheel itself had a retro cast to it, thanks to the banjo spoke design. The tweedy carpets and rich red leather seats and door trim recalled classic 1950s sports car styling. The instruments were grouped behind the steering wheel with silver facing and chrome bezels. The front windshield had a wraparound jet canopy feel.

The Pronto Spyder rode on seven-spoke 18-inch alloy wheels and was equipped for four-wheel disc brakes and ABS. The Spyder was one of the better-sorted drivers in Chrysler's concept car fleet. It was agile, quick, and fun to toss around. Jon Rundels, program executive for all of Chrysler's concept cars, reports that since its launch at the 1997 North American International Auto Show, the Pronto Spyder has been driven over 6,000 miles.

There were, however, a number of obstacles that stood between the Pronto Spyder and production. Not the least was the PET technology, which has yet to be adapted to automotive use for major body panels. The biggest issue that designers struggled with was whether the public was ready for a car that wasn't shiny. If a car with a matte finish is ever successfully marketed, it will dramatically alter the automotive landscape. The PET process was the key to Pronto Spyder's affordability, but failure of the matte finish to attract potential buyers could have prevented it from being a success.

The other obstacle was the phasing out of the Plymouth nameplate. Would the Pronto Spyder fit better with Dodge or Chrysler? On the one hand, Dodge with the Viper and its muscle car heritage is more about brute American power than European sporting machines. But a low-priced entry-level sports car didn't fit the Chrysler luxury car template. Ironically, Chrysler's earlier financial troubles may have made the Viper inevitable while the company's later success may have made the Pronto Spyder not worth doing.

Copperhead's dorsal fin was whittled down seven inches to its finished height. The fin theme picks up under the rear of the car. *John Lamm*

This sketch illustrates how the center stack on the Copperhead graphically represents a snake ready to strike. *Chrysler*

Interior detailing of Copperhead is intricate, laced with brushed aluminum and body-colored accents. *Chrysler, John Lamm*

The mid engined Pronto Spyder is as handsome as Porsche's Boxster but is amazingly targeted below $20,000, thanks to the plastic body and Neon powerplant. *Chrysler*

The Spyder interior is pure retro, from the banjo spokes of the steering wheel to the tweedy carpet pattern. White-faced instruments are surrounded by engine-turned bezels, while the pedals are made of brushed aluminum. Tortoise-shell is used for the wheel rim and shift knob. *Chrysler, John Lamm*

Designers wanted to call Pronto Spyder the "Gator" because of its toothy grille, slanted eyes, strong rear haunches, and slotted back. *John Lamm*

CHAPTER FIVE

AN ICON FOR CHRYSLER

Two of the best-known concept cars to go from show stand to city street are the Dodge Viper and Plymouth Prowler. Both will never be mistaken for basic transportation modules. They are about pure fun.

From Chrysler's point of view, however, the mission of a Dodge Viper or Plymouth Prowler is multifaceted. Sure they're fun and the car guys within the company certainly enjoy building and owning these cars. But more important, Viper and Prowler say something about the marque. These limited-run, high-impact cars serve to position a brand in the marketplace and provide styling cues for the rest of the cars in the line. You can see the cross-hatch grille of the Viper in the Ram truck, Stratus, and Intrepid. And it's no accident that Viper Red is the signature color of the division. Plymouth, which will cease to be a separate brand after 2001, used the Prowler's grille as an inspiration for the front end of the PT Cruiser. However, the decision to pull the plug on the brand resulted in the PT Cruiser being labeled a Chrysler prior to its launch.

Still, had Plymouth survived, you can bet that the Prowler cues would have been incorporated in future Voyager minivans and Breeze sedans.

Show cars that become limited-run production icons like Viper and Prowler also raise brand awareness by the free exposure on magazine covers, in newspaper articles, and on television. So if an icon is so important to a division, where is Chrysler's? "We've found it a few times," Gale admits, "but we just haven't built it yet."

Indeed, the company has looked long and hard for an icon that would serve its flagship brand, starting as early as 1991's Chrysler 300, coming virtually on the heels of the Viper. Using the V-10 under development for the Viper, the 300's inspiration came from the Monteverdi High Speed, a large four-door sedan built in Switzerland in the 1970s by Peter Monteverdi. Not coincidentally, Chrysler Hemi engines powered those legendary cars.

"The 300 was leveraging off the Viper," Lutz recalls. "We had all the hardware anyway. If we were ever going to

With its aggressive face, the Chrysler 300 projects the same in-your-face attitude as the Viper. *John Lamm*

do a luxury car, I felt we shouldn't do a dumb one, we should do a performance-oriented four-door sedan, and what came to mind was the Monteverdi High Speed sedan. In fact, we called the 300 the Monteverdi all the way through development."

That original Monteverdi High Speed had a feature that Lutz loved dearly—a driver's cockpit that was all business. "The driver's cell was done in all black with a black shell racing seat, a small leather-covered racing steering wheel, all the high-performance sports instrumentation, and the leather gearshift knob. The rest of the passenger compartment was in creamy Italian leather and burled walnut. I thought that was one of the best ideas I'd ever seen in terms of creating luxury transportation but saying the driver's area is serious business. So that was stolen for the 300, but it was stolen from a good source."

Lutz actually wanted to use the Monteverdi name on the concept car and called Peter Monteverdi to ask for permission. "I said, 'I would like to do this as a tribute to your years of leading edge design,' and he said, 'Well, what does that do for me?' I told him it would make him famous again. He said, 'I don't need fame, I'm famous enough.'" Lutz said he offered him a small honorarium, but Monteverdi countered with asking Chrysler to buy his company.

Lutz inquired, "What are you asking?" To which Monteverdi replied, "$13 million." And Lutz said, "Mr. Monteverdi, I think we'll figure out another name for our concept car."

Chrysler reached back into the 1950s and resurrected the 300 name. But while the original 300 was arguably the forerunner to the American muscle car, the 300 concept's body had a distinctively European flair. The shapely body, which was jokingly called cab rearward, was offset by a truly aggressive face. The 300 rode on a 125.9-inch wheelbase and was 206.5 inches long. It was wide (76.3 inches) and low at 51.2 inches. It was one of the first concept cars to ride on truly monstrous wheels. The fronts were 19 inches with P275/40 tires, while the rears were 20 inches shod with P335/35 rubber. Power came from the 8.0-liter Viper V-10, renamed the Copperhead V-10, which was tuned to produce 450 horsepower.

The 300 featured suicide doors and no B-pillar. The rear doors swung on massive circular discs carved from billet aluminum that served as hinges. Like the Monteverdi High Speed, the 300 featured a driver's cockpit done up in basic black, while the rest of the interior was clad in soft, tan leather with wood accents. Like the Viper, there were

In the 300's profile, the Viper-like sweep of the front and rear fenders is evident.
John Lamm

Inspired by the Monteverdi High Speed, the 300's cockpit is divided into two areas: the blacked-out driver's cell and the more luxurious passenger cabin done up in light tan leather. *John Lamm*

Dodge Viper's engine is pumped up to 450 horsepower and wears the Copperhead V-10 designation beneath the 300's hood. *John Lamm*

two hood-mounted ports and side exhausts, though the 300 kept the pipes hidden in the rockers and had subtle outlets positioned just below the rear doors.

The interior featured some James Bond touches, like a coded key card that was inserted in the center console, which then opened a door concealing an ignition button to push. The rear seating area was outfitted with a cellular phone, headphones, as well as a television and VCR.

Although the 300 was a show stopper, it was impractical to build. "It wasn't the greatest package candidate for a luxury car," Gale says. "It wouldn't have accepted a B-pillar very well without stretching it even more. It was already voluptuous and it would have looked like a limo had we stretched it more."

The B-pillar area was critical to having structure that could protect the car in a side-impact. To stretch the car or to build some sort of crash protection in the middle would have added weight and complexity to the product.

"I loved that car," Gale says. "It had kind of an OSCA grille and almost a boat-tail rear. It was so aggressive and it still looks great today."

Still, Gale doubts the Chrysler brand would have been ready for the 300 at the time. To him, the mechanicals were too close to the Viper, and Chrysler cars still needed their own specific theme or face. The OSCA-like grille, however, started the designers working in that direction.

The next attempt was the Thunderbolt, a rear-drive, V-8 powered coupe that resurrected its name from one of Chrysler's earliest concept cars, the 1941 Thunderbolt. The show car was a return to cab forward architecture, with a twist: the rear featured almost fastback styling with rear headroom coming from a double-bubble backlight.

The two-door approach fit in with the heritage of the Thunderbolt, but this modern concept car departed from the script by having a fixed head as opposed to the original's retractable hardtop.

The rear window of the Thunderbolt sports a double-bubble look to add a bit of rear-seat headroom in this rakish coupe. *Chrysler*

The floorpan beneath the Thunderbolt was LH but configured for rear-drive. This exercise was yet another attempt to explore the feasibility of converting that platform from front to rear-drive. As a result, the Thunderbolt rode on an independent suspension and was equipped with four-wheel disc brakes with ABS and traction control. The 4.0-liter 270-horsepower V-8 was an evolution of the powerplant used on the 1991 Optima, and it was mated to a four-speed automatic transmission.

The interior reflected the bubble shape of the canopy and the car was developed along a "pugnose" theme, according to Gale, though the grille opening was not as large as some later Chrysler studies. "As a car des-

tined for production? No, we wouldn't have done it," Gale says. "It was part of a library or catalog of design themes we were developing. What you have to do is stake out enough turf, so that maybe you can come back and do something like it later."

Thunderbolt and some of the cars that followed were used to pull styling elements or cues for use on production cars rather than trying to do a modern flagship or icon. Wheel themes, the curve of a fender, the shape of a grille, or even the design of a badge were elements that migrated to Chrysler's volume models. In a micro sense, this was the impact of the ongoing search for an icon for the Chrysler brand.

In a macro sense, something else was happening as the thinking on concept cars was evolving in a different direction. Rather than being a stepping stone to production, the concept cars being developed under the Chrysler nameplate were letting the world know that, in an era where bean counters were calling the shots for the competition, car guys still ruled at Chrysler. The message from these retro dream cars was simple: Chrysler is uniquely qualified to build the best-looking cars on the market because it understands the industry's past. It was a bold proposition, but how else do you explain the Chrysler Atlantic?

"We did the Atlantic because it was just so outrageous," Gale says of the 1995 concept car. Both he and Lutz were judges at the Pebble Beach Concours d' Elegance. At that show, in addition to the classic cars competing for best-in-show honors on the 18th fairway, Concours organizers began to exhibit vintage and current concept cars on the upper lawn behind the Lodge. "This is one of those deals where we decided that the next year we were going to put everyone who had cars on the upper lawn on the trailer. That was our goal, whether it took 21- or 22-inch wheels, if it took forms inspired by the 1930s French coachbuilders. We had to invent this thing and we were determined to pull it off."

Legend has it that Lutz sketched the Atlantic on a cocktail napkin. Gale still has those doodles, but he never showed them to his design staff. "We described what we wanted to do with words, but I would never take the sketch down to the studio," Gale confides. "What will happen is that they [the designers] will step back and you lose all their creative input. They'll say, 'Hey, he's got all the answers.' You can't set up that kind of atmosphere. You can go in there and bend it and get it the way you want it, which is the way we operate."

The Atlantic was retro at its finest. It faithfully recalled the teardrop-shaped Talbot-Lago and Bugatti Atlantic Coupes of the 1930s and was a major hit of the 1995 North American International Auto Show. A rolling piece of sculpture designed by Bob Hubbach, the Atlantic rode

Thunderbolt touts cab forward design, but its clean front end bears no relationship to future Chrysler styling themes. *John Lamm*

Despite its radical exterior shape, the Thunderbolt's interior design is fairly conventional. *John Lamm*

Part of Atlantic's appeal is the fact that it's built to be driven. *John Lamm*

on a 126-inch wheelbase and had an overall length of 199.5 inches. Again, in keeping with the lower, longer, wider school of design, the car was 75.8 inches wide and 51.6 inches tall. The wheels were huge, 21 inches in the front and 22 inches in the rear.

Everything from the design (the flowing shapes of the fenders and the fore-to-aft spline line down the center of the vehicle) to the hardware under the hood (it had a 325-horsepower straight eight, created from two 2.0-liter four-cylinder Neon engines) harkened back to an earlier time. Still, there was much that was modern about the Atlantic, including its four-wheel disc brakes with ABS, AutoStick automatic transmission, and the use of neon lighting for the center high-mounted stoplight, rear brake lights, and interior dome lighting. Inside, the neutral and dark rose-

Atlantic's boat-tail rear end sports a center spline that echoes the classic Bugatti Atlantic. *John Lamm*

wood leather skins were offset by gold-trimmed watch-face type instrumentation (which was later adapted to the production LHS).

"You probably can't find a period in history like the late 1930s with a stronger statement of incredibly romantic, image-leading coupes," Gale said when the Atlantic was unveiled. And while there were thoughts of maybe a very limited production run, they were dismissed early as unrealistic. An icon for Chrysler would have to be a four-door.

"The two-door market as we used to know it is gone," says Gale. "Sedans really do everything that the coupe used to do. They're sporty and aggressive, and you don't need a two-door to express yourself anymore. And that's too bad because we're losing an automotive art form."

The Chrysler Phaeton, which bowed two years later, was conceived with virtually the same Pebble Beach game plan in mind. This time, Lutz says, the Phaeton had much to do with "my fascination with metal hardtops that go away. And that goes back to when I was eight and I saw the Thunderbolt, and its flap opened up and I saw that metal top disappear. I thought that was the cat's meow."

Gale also sees the Phaeton as "a deliberate, overt American form. But it also staked out some of the graphics we use on production cars." It also draws on the heritage of Chrysler's 1941 Newport Dual Cowl Phaeton image car. The round, gently curved fenders and body forms of the Phaeton are punctuated by sharp creases. "It's like having a great pair of pants with a perfect crease," Gale observes.

The dual-cowl Phaeton was a monster. With a 132-inch wheelbase, the car measured 215 inches in overall length and was 78 inches wide and 55 inches tall. It rode on 22-inch wheels with P245/55R22 tires. The two-piece hardtop electrically stowed in the trunk. Power came from a 5.4-liter 48-valve V-12, which produced 425 horsepower.

The Phaeton sported two windshields and the second cowl housed its own speedometer and tachometer so the rear seat passengers could monitor the car's performance. The leather-clad seats front and rear were more like overstuffed

Atlantic's 4.0-liter straight-eight engine is actually two 2.0-liter Neon four-cylinder engines joined together. *John Lamm*

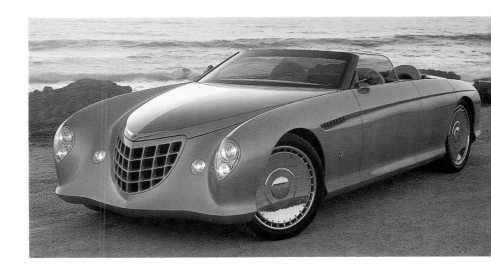

The dual-cowl Phaeton incorporates a hardtop that disappears with the touch of a button. Note the retractable windscreen on the rear cowl. *John Lamm*

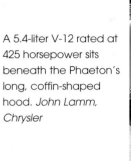

A 5.4-liter V-12 rated at 425 horsepower sits beneath the Phaeton's long, coffin-shaped hood. *John Lamm, Chrysler*

The four-passenger Phaeton uses conventional hinges instead of a suicide door design popularized on other show cars. *John Lamm*

club chairs with armrests and handy consoles than traditional buckets. The interior was also finished with satin metal accents and Zebrano wood inlays.

Still, the Phaeton was not a producible icon like Viper or Prowler. "There's a big difference between doing a Viper or Prowler and doing an icon for Chrysler," Lutz explains. "The Viper Roadster, Viper Coupe, and Prowler are all cars where you don't need world class levels of refinement, fit and finish, automatic climate control systems, premium sound systems, wonderful door latches, and everything that fits perfectly. In a Viper Roadster or a Viper Coupe, which are essentially street legal extreme performance cars, the customer is not that focused on the

Inspired by Virgil Exner's 1953 d'Elegance, the Chronos is the closest a Chrysler icon has come to production. *John Lamm*

slickness of details. The same thing is true for the Prowler. The minute you go into a luxury sedan—and that was the problem with the Atlantic and the Phaeton—people pay attention to that stuff."

Instead, cars like the Atlantic and the Phaeton incorporated some sort of heraldry that would be used on the production cars. The Atlantic's winged badge is an example of a design element that was conceived and then refined and put to use on all Chrysler products.

The Chronos would be different. Designed for the 1998 North American International Auto Show, the Chronos was inspired by legendary Chrysler designer Virgil Exner's 1953 d'Elegance, which was crafted with the help of noted Italian design house Ghia.

"This time," Lutz says of Chronos, "we decided not to do one that was pie in the sky, and if we decided to do it for real, we'd have to start all over again. This time at every step of the design we were mindful of the possibility of future production. And so Chronos was closest to what you could actually do in a production car. Obviously we would have had to modify it a bit—the wheels would have to get a little smaller, the hood would have to get a little shorter, the DLO [daylight opening] would have to get a little higher. But I think we could have kept the essence of the car. All the designers, European and American alike, were captivated with that car. Some of the Italian designers said the surfaces, the lines, and the proportion were close to perfection. We reached into the past with the Virgil Exner designs and yet it was all new."

Osamu Shikado and Jack Crain designed the Chronos and gave it larger-than-life proportions with the 131-inch wheelbase. The almost square, egg-crate grille of the Chronos was a pure Chrysler form of the 1950s and yet was integrated nicely into the flowing bodywork. That

Designers from around the world praised Chronos for its spectacular surface development. The rear fenders are works of art. *John Lamm*

grille echoed the current LHS and even a bit of the 1991 300 show car. Instead of using a Viper V-10, the designers and engineers working on Chronos made a new dohc power plant by adding two cylinders to the 4.7-liter Jeep V-8. Displacement was 6.0 liters and the engine produced about 350 horsepower. If the Chronos had gone into production, it would have most likely been powered by a V-8.

The 20-inch wheels featured unique center spinners that remained level while the wheels turned. Also of note was that the Chrysler seal, a trademark dating to the earliest days of the company, was resurrected on the Chronos and adapted for production cars.

Inside, the design was uncluttered but not spare. The instruments had the jeweled look of a fine watch. There were wood and metal accents and seats trimmed luxuriously in leather. The long wheelbase meant that the rear seat passengers had limousine-like accommodations. The Chronos was outfitted to be the perfect chauffeur-driven mobile office. One touch that cigar aficionado Bob Lutz appreciated was a center console equipped with a humidor.

Though the high beltline gave the car a low and long elegant look from the outside, from the driver's seat there was almost a pill-box effect when it came to visibility. The V-10 was strong and burbled nicely through a Borla low-restriction exhaust. Though the Chronos was driveable, its role as a luxury cruiser didn't invite hard driving. It was quiet, powerful, almost subdued. Yet in its own way, the stunning good looks of the Chronos would have made it an ideal flagship for the Chrysler fleet. That is, until the merger with Daimler-Benz.

"We gave up on it because at that point the issue of doing a future flagship for Chrysler, where we could legitimately bring back the Imperial name, went to sleep because we were already in heavy talks with Daimler," Lutz says. "Why should we move the Chrysler brand up to challenge the world's finest luxury cars when we would be linked with the world's finest luxury cars?"

So will Chrysler get an icon like the Viper? Maybe not. Still, Gale believes these cars, from the 300 right through to the Chronos, had a profound effect on Chrysler's image, even if they never made it into production.

"We were always inching the Chrysler image up. It was really part of our strategy and concept cars deserve credit," Gale says. From building heavily rebated cars like the New Yorker and Imperial with their waterline belts to the current production 300M and LHS, which carry forms, cues, and badging from these concept cars, the image of Chrysler luxury has been transformed.

"The proof of this success," Gale explains, "is that since we have been doing this, Chrysler has a higher average revenue per vehicle than its domestic competitors. Given from where we came from, it is almost inconceivable."

Yet the search for an icon continues.

Understatement is the key to elegance in Chronos' interior. Minimal instrumentation and major controls hidden by aluminum-colored panels give the dash the look of a fine piece of furniture. *John Lamm*

Although the Chronos is V-10 powered, it's not the Viper's pushrod engine beneath the hood, but rather a 4.7-liter Jeep dohc V-8 with two extra cylinders and 6.0 liters of displacement. *John Lamm*

CHAPTER SIX

SEARCHING FOR A PERFECT JEEP

While some of Chrysler's concepts cars of the 1990s were calculated risks to condition the public (and even upper management) to radically styled future products, or to make big statements about a brand's image, others were simply studies designed to probe for potential hot spots among an unsuspecting public.

But, as Bob Lutz puts it in his book *Guts*, you can listen to the voice of the customer for only so long. In fact, Lutz believes that the customer isn't always right. He writes: "I've seen too many customers who hadn't a clue about what they wanted, or worse, who deliberately fibbed when the nice survey-taker with the clipboard asked them what they'd like…Sometimes they want something they can't yet express. When they see it, though, they buy it."

Concept cars provide a relatively low-cost way to look for these opportunities—and allow designers to have some fun along the way.

Over time, many of these studies turned out to be Jeeps. It was not by any grand design, but simply because the Jeep brand lent itself perfectly to such experimentation. Of all the nameplates in Chrysler's stable, Jeep was the strongest and most consistent performer. Its name is a household word. The SUV market was set to explode and Jeep had a lock on the rugged, boxy styling theme that defined this segment.

"The Koreans or the Japanese would love to have the imagery associated with the Jeep," Gale says. "Everybody is out there nipping around the edges of the sport-ute market and it is Jeep's style they want to steal."

Because of such a strong market position, there wasn't a pressing need for Jeep to have concept vehicles to predict future styling or to talk about future products. For Jeep, the future was now with the Wrangler and Cherokee, vehicles that were popular precisely because the styling hadn't changed.

The only exception was its Concept 1, which was launched in 1988 (some eight years before Volkswagen showed its Concept 1 prototype for the New Beetle). It was

The adjustable suspension raises the Jeepster four inches to improve off-road ground clearance.
John Lamm

Sketches of the Ecco envision a smaller, more environmentally friendly Jeep aimed primarily at the European market. Chrysler

Glen Abbott

Inside, Ecco's center-mounted instrumentation can be adapted to either left or right-hand drive. *John Lamm*

The finished Ecco show car is smaller than the current Wrangler and sports a car-like greenhouse. *John Lamm*

a thinly disguised Grand Cherokee, which was slated to replace the eight-year-old Cherokee. The company had a lot riding on this new sport-ute, called the ZJ, not the least being $1 billion in a new assembly plant on Detroit's east side. Chrysler wanted to give the public a preview of what was coming. To cover its bets while the ZJ was ramping up, Chrysler decided to keep the Cherokee around for maybe a year. ZJ was a hit, but a strange thing happened: Cherokee sales held up and the vehicle continues in production today. The Cherokee's survival would later save a future concept vehicle, the Dakar, from the scrap heap.

In 1991, Jeep had its first pure concept vehicle in the Wagoneer 2000, a huge, almost banana-shaped sport-ute. "We frequently did not do good concepts for Jeep," Lutz recalls. "There was a genuine purpose in the Dodge truck stuff, in the small car stuff, and in all the things derived from Portofino. There was rarely any broader predictive Jeep stuff other than the Jeep brand guys saying, 'Hey, if Plymouth is going to have a concept car on the stand and Dodge is and Chrysler is and Dodge Truck is, how about us?'

"Then design would say, 'Oh yeah, you guys deserve one too.' And it would get very little management attention, except a little thought in the backs of our minds to find a way that we could bring the Grand Wagoneer back. In other words, do a full-size sport-utility again. That was what the Wagoneer 2000 was about, but it was huge, with big silly wheels. I just wasn't that fond of it."

Riding on 20-inch wheels, the Jeep Wagoneer 2000 had a Hummer-like width of 80 inches and stood 67.5 inches tall. It rode on a 138-inch wheelbase and was 198.1 inches in overall length. Unlike boxy Jeeps, the Wagoneer had a curved and rounded body with a rather large snout. Its proportions were almost ungainly.

In fact, the Wagoneer 2000 was a better interior than exterior study. Inside, the front and rear bench seats had detachable center units that could be positioned behind the rear bench for unique 2+2+2 seating. These smaller units sported wings that folded out to convert them into standard size seats. The Wagoneer was also outfitted with a unique entertainment center, which included television, VCR, and compact disc player that moved on a track down the center of the vehicle between the six passengers. And the rear tailgate was equipped with removable stadium seats.

Interesting external detailing included a flush-mounted pop-up roof rack, a built-in trailer hitch, and built-in steps that pulled out of the door sills.

In 1993, the Jeep Ecco bowed. Incorporating many of the advanced engineering ideas of Francois Castaing, the Ecco was developed with an eye toward making a small Jeep that was totally recyclable. The vehicle was made entirely of aluminum and plastic and had a shape that was cute and huggable.

"This little Jeep was kind of the companion to the Neon," Castaing says. "Even though we were not sure the

The sliding canvas roof is equipped with a pop-up feature along the backlight to provide additional headroom for Ecco's rear seat passengers. *Chrysler*

The drooping long snout of Wagoneer 2000 lacks the strength needed to convey the ruggedness of a full-size sport-utility vehicle. *John Lamm*

The Jeep Concept 1's blacked-out glass and headlamps thinly disguise the all-new Grand Cherokee. *Chrysler*

two-stroke would ever work, and we were not too sure the market was ready for advanced technology for the sake of ecology, I felt strongly that alongside the big monster Chrysler 300, with 400 horsepower and huge 21-inch wheels, we should balance that out with other products that were more friendly to people."

And like the Neon, Ecco used a two-stroke 1.5-liter (up from 1.1 liters) aluminum three-cylinder engine that made 85 horsepower and 120 lb-ft of torque. Riding on 16-inch wheels, the Ecco stood on a compact 100.3-inch wheelbase and was only 143 inches in overall length. Still, the Ecco was tall and wide, measuring a respective 64.7 and 70.6 inches. It combined the rugged lower body of a Jeep with a greenhouse that was rounded like that of the French Citroen 2CV, which wasn't coincidental. Like the Citroen, the Ecco featured a folding canvas sunroof that popped up like a tent in the back to improve headroom for the rear passengers during inclement weather. It was equipped with a six-speed manual transaxle mounted amidships that provided drive to all four wheels.

"Jeep designers kept exploring this concept of a smaller, lighter version of the Wrangler," Lutz explains. "We in America look at the Wrangler and see a small- to medium-size vehicle, but when you see it in a European context, it's an absolute monster. It looks gigantic in Europe. There is a lot of latent demand in Europe for a light, small, environmentally friendly vehicle with a Jeep badge and Jeep characteristics.

"The problem is one of investments," he notes. "You have to make it lower priced, yet in terms of cost, it would be much the same as the Wrangler. The other consideration is that the Wrangler is a very profitable vehicle and if you do something underneath it at a lower profit that is more attractive, you're going to kill this very profitable thing. So you need to be very careful that you don't shoot yourself in the foot. In the United States, where we do believe that size matters, it (Ecco) was just OK. But the

Jeep Icon explores design themes of future Wranglers. It remains true to the Jeep tradition with its seven-slat grille and round headlamps. Beneath the skin, however, is a transversely mounted four-cylinder engine. *Chrysler*

Europeans just loved it. They grooved on that thing."

More studies of the future direction of Jeep were undertaken in 1997 and 1998 with the Icon and Jeepster. The Icon was an attempt to do a Wrangler makeover for the 2000s. Unlike the Wagoneer 2000, the Icon's shape remained fairly faithful to the traditional Jeep look.

"We have a responsibility as caretakers of one of the world's most recognized brands," explains Trevor Creed, Chrysler's design director. "Sooner or later we will be challenged with freshening Jeep Wrangler's appearance without sacrificing its distinctive image and instantly recognizable characteristics."

The Icon, at 142 inches, was 5 inches shorter while standing on the same 93.4-inch wheelbase of the current Wrangler. Icon was also wider, had shorter front and rear

overhangs and 2 inches more suspension travel for its 19-inch wheels. The Icon incorporated such retro Jeep styling touches as a flat-folding front windshield, round headlamps, and exposed hood latches.

As a concept, the Icon departed from Jeep tradition by using a transversely mounted 150 horsepower 2.4-liter four-cylinder engine mated to a six-speed Autostick transaxle. But in keeping with Jeep's heritage, the driveline had two ranges, high and low, which provided 12 gears.

The Icon was also constructed as an aluminum-intensive study. The safety cage and body frame were made of aluminum, as were the seats, which used aluminum tubes covered with waterproof leather upholstery.

"We kept the exposed hinges, bold bumpers, exposed door handles, and gas cap, which were designed to give the vehicle more of a mechanical, industrial design feel and at the same time add a lot of intrinsic value," Creed says. "Where the vehicle differed the most is that it was designed as unibody construction with an integrated aluminum roll cage" as opposed to the Wrangler's body-on-frame construction.

Icon designer Robert Laster says his inspiration for the Icon wasn't other SUVs but mountain bikes. "Just like top-of-the-line mountain bikes, Icon was built to go anywhere. Its parts are high quality, lightweight, and purpose-built. To communicate the quality of each part, we branded our Jeep logo on the hinges, door handles, wheels, and bumpers."

While the concept behind the Icon was pretty true to Jeep's off-roading tradition, the Jeepster, first shown in 1998, was more of an anything-goes attempt to infuse the SUV market with sports car attitude.

Mike Moore, Chrysler's chief designer of Jeep products, calls it a 'what if' exercise: "What if you could have the power and excitement of a sports car coupled with the capability and rugged go-anywhere nature of a Jeep Wrangler?"

Moore says the designers initially penned the Jeepster as a two-seater. But after Gale reviewed the design it was decided that the vehicle would be more practical as a 2+2. Moore notes the additional length needed to convert the vehicle helped its overall proportions.

"We originally codenamed the vehicle 'Project Grizzly.' But we decided to search Jeep heritage and settled on Jeepster, from the rare and now quite collectible 1950 Willys Jeep Convertible," Moore observes.

Though it was just a fun exercise, the Jeepster benefited from the latest in Chrysler concept car thinking. It had to be a runner and it had to be detailed as though it was producible.

The Jeepster promised brute power from its 4.7-liter V-8, which was tuned to produce 300 horsepower. The engine was a sneak peek at the powerplant that would be used in the next generation Jeep Grand Cherokee, set for a 1999 launch. A four-speed automatic transmission with viscous coupling and on-demand four-wheel drive was mated to the engine. The two-door convertible had a unit-body steel chassis and rode on a 106-inch wheelbase with an overall length of 142 inches. It stood 58 inches tall and had a width of 71 inches.

The Jeepster's roof retracted in the rear, the roof pillars and rails remained fixed. The Jeepster wore huge 19x9-inch wheels with P255/55R19 Goodyear Extended Mobility Tires, which meant no spare.

The highly detailed interior was styled to look like a military radio with such touches as round gauges with white faces. There was also an extensive use of anodized aluminum accents, giving the interior a highly functional machined look. The seats, with their cognac-colored leather inserts, used the same kind of water-repellant skins used on hiking boots and featured four-point safety harnesses.

One functional aspect on the Jeepster that will likely be incorporated in future Jeeps was the adjustable ride height suspension. The electronic four-wheel independent suspension raised and lowered the body via a console switch. In normal mode, the Jeepster had a ground clearance of 5.75 inches. By hitting the switch, ground clear-

Icon's aluminum theme is carried into the cabin with exposed tubing on the seatbacks and aluminum-finished bezels on the instrument panel. Instrumentation is again center-mounted. *Chrysler*

ance was increased by four inches, further enhancing the ability of the vehicle, which had short overhangs to begin with, to traverse rocks and other obstructions off-road.

Unfortunately, as a business proposition, the Jeepster was a nonstarter. There was no pressing need to further burnish the Jeep brand with an icon like Jeepster. Even though it used a shortened Grand Cherokee platform, it was difficult to make a business case to build such a low-volume model in the Jeep range.

That wasn't the case with the Dakar, a 1997 concept of a four-door Wrangler. It seemed like a natural. Two doors were added by stretching the Wrangler's wheelbase almost 15 inches to 108.5 inches. "With a longer wheelbase, we were able to offer additional space for passengers and their gear," says Creed. "We were also able to further improve the ride by positioning backseat passengers in

The Jeepster's convertible top slides into the rear cargo area along the fixed sills. The twin center exhaust is a Viper design cue. *Chrysler*

The Jeepster's interior styling theme mimics the design of military radios by using circular instruments with white faces. Aluminum-colored Allen bolts add to the look. *John Lamm*

front of the rear axle as opposed to directly on top of it."

Though the front clip was essentially the same as the Wrangler, with its round headlamps and seven-slot grille, Dakar incorporated a new windshield and side glass, new door designs, and a steel roof.

The roof offered the advantage of being fitted with a full-length built-in tubular rack, a manual canvas sliding sunroof, four front-mounted rally lamps, strategically placed grab handles, and roof-mounted spare tire.

Adding to the rugged, off-road look of the Dakar were Jeep's signature exposed hinges and hood latches as well as full-length running boards, an externally mounted shovel on the front fender, and gas cans built onto the rear tailgate. A special "adventure kit" was integrated into the rear door and contained a night vision scope, binoculars, flashlight, and compass.

Inside, the dash was stock Wrangler, but the accents added a touch of luxury. "We utilized wood and leather to give the interior of the vehicle more of a civilized, European-styled flavor," Creed explains. The earth-toned cabin was outfitted with a wood-trimmed steering wheel and door inserts, soft woven leather seating surfaces, and tightly wound Berber carpeting.

Though the wheelbase and 166.5-inch overall length of the Dakar was greater than the Wrangler, most of the other dimensions remained the same, including the 75-inch width and—this is rare for concept vehicles—stock wheels and tires that measured only 15 inches in diameter.

The Dakar employed the same steel body-on-frame construction as the Wrangler. It also shared the same suspension and braking system, which used front discs and rear drums. In fact, Dakar looked so production-ready, the buzz around the 1997 show was that Chrysler would be in production with the four-door within 18 months. But it wasn't to be, at least for the time being.

"We could have done the Dakar three or four years earlier," Lutz says. "We would have put it into production for not a lot of money; some $300 to $350 million would

When the suspension is in the down position, the Jeepster looks like a lowrider. *John Lamm*

have gotten us that vehicle." The problem was that there was a lot of internal resistance to doing a third Jeep platform for the company's Toledo assembly plant that builds the Wrangler and the Cherokee.

"The only reason for not doing the Dakar was that the Wrangler was essentially sold out anyway," Lutz explains. "If it wasn't going to be substitutional, we were going to have to figure where do we put it and that would have triggered a lot more investment." So despite the positive response to the Dakar, it was unlikely that one would be built off the Wrangler.

But Lutz also firmly believed there was a spot in the market for a rugged four-door sport-ute like the Dakar. "The sport-utility market is starting to fragment more than just by size. It's starting to fragment by personality," Lutz believes. "There are the slick semi-car ones, the huge get-out-of-my-way Navigators and Expeditions, and the in-between-size Grand Cherokees and Cherokees. There's this type that has not been exploited in the United States, the purely functional kind inspired by Land Rover. There is no American Land Rover with the stiff sides and the big luggage rack and the place to put gasoline cans or carry an exposed spare wheel."

At about the same time, the designers were working on a replacement for the Cherokee (codenamed XJ), which had been around since 1984 with only minor makeovers. For the new one, known as KJ, the studios were trying to do a modern SUV. The problem, according

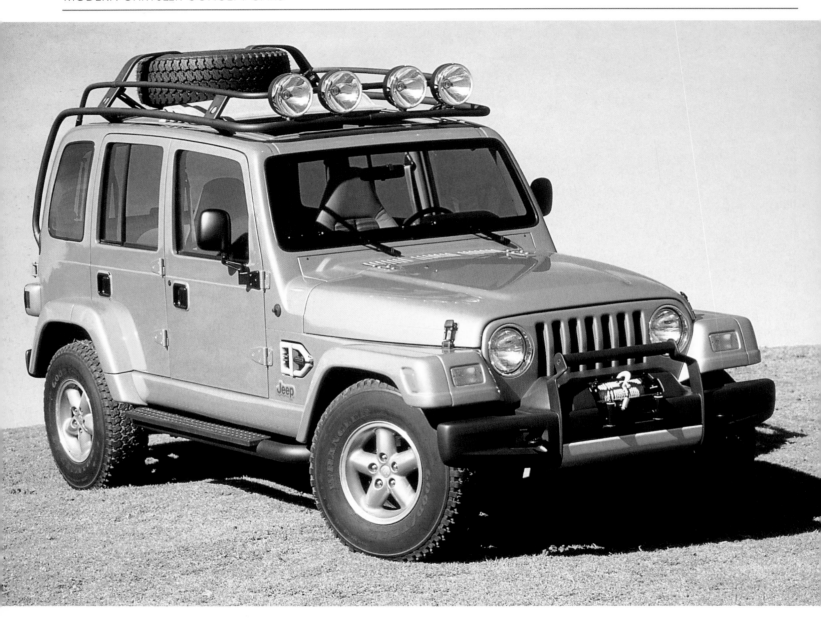

Jeep Dakar explored the idea of doing a four-door Wrangler with minimal investment. *Chrysler*

to Lutz, is that the studies kept looking like a slightly smaller version of the recently introduced Grand Cherokee, the WJ.

"I told them that you could hardly tell them apart. The WJ is a little bigger and the KJ was just a little smaller," Lutz says. "The Grand Cherokee was going to be a replacement for the Cherokee. They were going to be the same size, weight, and cost. As it happened, instead of killing the Cherokee, we were going to reprice it and reposition it and run it in parallel with the Grand Cherokee for a few months until we got production ramped up. Then we began to understand that if we kept pricing the Cherokee right, it would have a life of its own and in the final analysis was going to be a better value than a Toyota RAV4 and all that stuff. We realized the XJ isn't going away; we're selling 175,000 a year worldwide, why put it to sleep?

"We never did a careful segment analysis that said the world wants one Cherokee that's a little bigger and round and one Cherokee that's a little smaller and square," Lutz confides. "We lucked into this. Now that we have the opportunity to do it over, why try to make them as similar as possible when they are going to be almost the same size? We'd end up doing what so many of the Japanese and General Motors keep doing over and over again: doing two vehicles for the public where they say, 'Why'd they do that?' If it's too close to the Grand Cherokee it will just cannibalize sales. Why not use this opportunity to make the Cherokee something entirely different? That's what we did with the Dakar design. We moved the Dakar design over into the next Cherokee."

The transplant was not a literal translation. The design has evolved somewhat because the Cherokee is a unit body vehicle, while the Wrangler is body-on-frame. The primary benefit is a vehicle that is nearly 500 pounds lighter. And still, the cues from the show

Although the exterior is utilitarian, the Dakar is European upscale on the inside, with wood accents and leather-trimmed seats. *Chrysler*

car remain. Gale believes that if the next Cherokee is dressed up like the Dakar, people will be hard pressed to tell the difference.

"Dakar lives," Lutz says with satisfaction. "It did its job, getting a myopic group of people to see outside. There is a place for a truly functional, off-road-looking four-door in the Jeep line-up. The next XJ will be a smash hit."

The Dakar may prove that it isn't the customer that is always right, but rather the concept.

BRANCHING OUT

The premiere venue for unveiling Chrysler concept cars has been the North American International Auto Show in Detroit. But in 1996, the company took the unusual step of unveiling two truck concepts at the Specialty Equipment Marketers Association meeting in Las Vegas. SEMA, as it's known, was initially an association of speed equipment suppliers and tuners. It has since evolved into a highly diversified trade group for all after-market customization.

Using the engine from the Viper, Dodge showcased the Sidewinder, a hot rod pickup with retro T-bucket cues. "The Sidewinder was sort of a sneak peak of what we were going to do with the Dakota, especially the grille treatment and the front fenders," Gale says. The Dakota had been a conventional looking, boxy pickup, but its redesign would give it a fendered look similar to the Ram.

The Sidewinder was painted a tangerine metalflake and had a one-piece box with fenders that matched those on the front of the vehicle. A convertible with a removable hardtop, the Sidewinder also had a hard tonneau cover for the box to give it an even sportier look. Inside, the dash, transmission hump, and door panels were body-colored metal. The instruments were arranged in three circles, with the tach in front of the driver and a center circle that housed the gas and water temperature gauges as well as the radio controls. The third circle, with the speedometer, was in front of the passenger. The center shifter was done in brushed aluminum and the controls for the heating and air conditioning were also console-mounted. The whimsy of this pickup hot rod was communicated in a gas pedal shaped like a bare foot and marked "go" while the conventional brake pedal was stamped "whoa." The turn signal indicators were named Louie and Ralph.

Making its Vegas debut alongside the Sidewinder was the Dodge T-Rex, the ultimate Ram pickup with a 500-horsepower V-10 and six-wheel drive. T-Rex stands for Technology Research Experimental vehicle.

"Our intention was to develop a personal vehicle that could out-tow, out-off-road, out-maneuver, out-haul, and out-run anything in its class," says Leong C. Dong, manager of chassis/drivetrain in Chrysler's advance vehicle engineering truck group.

More of a mechanical than design exercise, the T-Rex used a tandem rear wheel layout to achieve the same load-carrying capacity of a single axle

Dodge Sidewinder projects a hot rod attitude on a midsize pickup platform. At the same time, it previews the look of the second-generation Dakota pickup. *Chrysler*

Billed as the ultimate Dodge Ram, the T-Rex 6x6 coaxes 500 horsepower from its V-10 engine. *Chrysler*

dual rear-wheel truck but, because of the narrow track, it would have better maneuverability and a tighter turning circle. And by driving all six wheels, the T-Rex was expected to have tremendous off-road capability.

The drivetrain featured a five-position electric shift offering full-time four-wheel drive on the rear axles and full- or part-time six-wheel drive with the front axle engaged. The system also incorporated an external transfer case behind the second axle to send power to the third axle. The Magnum V-10 was modified with high-compression pistons, a billet crank, ported and polished heads, a modified camshaft, and tubular headers to boost output from 360 horsepower to 500 and torque from 450 ft-lb to 600. The T-Rex was a quick monster. Dodge reported 0-60 miles per hour acceleration of 7.7 seconds, a quarter mile in 16.1 seconds at 88 miles per hour, and 50-70 miles per hour passing in 4.5 seconds.

With a gross vehicle weight rating of 12,000 pounds, the T-Rex could carry a 5,000-pound payload and tow up to 26,000 pounds.

The cargo box on the T-Rex was a half-foot longer than a standard eight-foot bed to accommodate the two rear axles and was clad in a molded Kevlar and carbon fiber skin.

The T-Rex also had an adaptive air-suspension system located by the trailing arms and track bar, with automatic load leveling as well as controls to lower the vehicle to ease entry and exit as well as a high setting for increased ground clearance in off-road situations.

In 1999, the company returned to SEMA with the Howler, a Prowler that was modified to accept a Jeep 4.7-liter V-8 and a five-speed manual transmission. By replacing the four-speed rear-mounted transaxle with the conventionally mounted manual, the Prowler's rear end was opened up to accommodate a pick-up style cargo box as well as a larger gas tank.

Howler was actually two projects in one. Jon Rundels, concept and specialty vehicle executive, was looking for a way to answer critics who said the Prowler should have had a V-8 instead of a V-6. Meanwhile, designer Christopher Schuttera, two years out of the University of Cincinnati, had an idea of marrying the classic form of a pickup with a sporty two-seater.

"Here we had two enthusiast projects going in our own Auburn Hills studios that you would expect to see in an automotive specialty shop," Gale says. "What better place than the

By stretching the wheelbase 20 inches, the Howler is able to accommodate a 4.7-liter V-8 instead of the Prowler's stock V-6. *Chrysler*

SEMA show, which is all about customization and conversion, to link these projects and create another stunning show car?"

Rundels' team swapped out the V-6 with the Jeep 4.7-liter V-8. While the V-8 made 250 horsepower, a little less than the 253 horsepower from the 3.5-liter V-6, it offered far more torque: 300 ft-lb compared to 255. The rear transaxle was traded for an engine-mounted five-speed Borg Warner T-5 manual transmission. The pedal package from the stock Prowler was replaced with a three-pedal cluster, including clutch, from the Neon. Removing the transaxle provided the opportunity to reposition the gas tank, which previously had taken up most of the trunk area of the Prowler.

"This allowed us to open up the rear of the car and create space for a trunk while leaving the front end, doors, and interior unchanged," Schuttera says. "The result is a show car that remains true to the heritage of the home-built hot rod, yet offers true everyday convenience."

As part of the conversion, the wheelbase was stretched 20 inches to 133.3 inches. With the wheels so far forward, the front bumpers were removed. Other changes included substituting a power hardtop for the manual soft top and using a lockable hard tonneau cover for the rear cargo box.

Later at the same SEMA show, Chrysler announced that it would be phasing out the Plymouth brand by 2002, meaning that the Prowler would be discontinued. As a result, the Howler remains a one-off, unless the market decides that it really needs a hot rod with a pickup box.

CHAPTER SEVEN

TECHNOLOGY RULES

Tucked away in a nondescript light industrial park in Madison Heights, Michigan, Chrysler's Liberty group toils away in obscurity. Far from the klieg lights of the exhibition halls with little or no chance that its work will be splashed across magazine covers or in newspapers, this group of engineers has been doing a concept car a year for the last 10 years. The public has seen maybe three of them.

Welcome to Liberty.

Formed in the early 1980s by Lee Iacocca, Liberty was charged with developing a low-cost import-fighting small car to replace the aging Omni/Horizon. Though Liberty promised to be a car, it became more of a process, with its focus shifted to advanced product development. By the time Francois Castaing joined the company in 1987 with the AMC acquisition, Liberty was responsible for doing the early development work for the LH sedans. At that time, Liberty was working out of another anonymous light industrial complex on Featherstone Road in Auburn Hills, not far from where Chrysler's sprawling technical center and headquarters would be built.

Instead of handing LH work over to Large Car engineering in Highland Park, Castaing moved the newly formed LH platform team, which was headed by Glenn Gardner, to Featherstone Road. Liberty, in turn, decamped to Madison Heights where it was taken over by Tom Moore, a former Ford engineer. There, Liberty took on a new challenge.

"Tom's charter was to produce one new, breakthrough concept vehicle per year," Castaing says. "I didn't believe in pure research per se, because people can work forever on a concept and it may never materialize, much less get packaged into the constraint of a car." By imposing the discipline of actually building one vehicle per year, there was a practical bent to Liberty's work.

While concepts like the Epic minivan and the Neon-based Aviat employed Liberty-developed technology, two

Patriot looks like a conventional Le Mans racer, but beneath its Reynard chassis is a giant flywheel and gas-fired turbine delivering energy to powerful electric motors. *Chrysler*

91

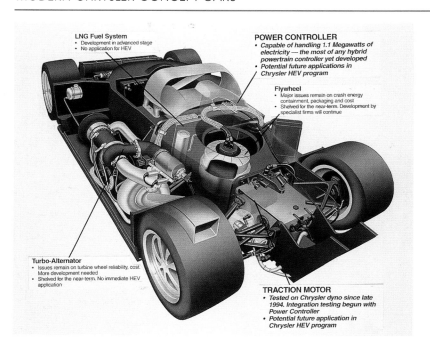

LNG Fuel System
• Development in advanced stage
• No application for HEV

POWER CONTROLLER
• Capable of handling 1.1 Megawatts of electricity — the most of any hybrid powertrain controller yet developed
• Potential future applications in Chrysler HEV program

Flywheel
• Major issues remain on crash energy containment, packaging and cost
• Shelved for the near-term. Development by specialist firms will continue

Turbo-Alternator
• Issues remain on turbine wheel reliability, cost. More development needed
• Shelved for the near-term. No immediate HEV application

TRACTION MOTOR
• Tested on Chrysler dyno since late 1994. Integration testing begun with Power Controller
• Potential future application in Chrysler HEV program

The major systems on board Patriot are detailed in this cutaway. The project was abandoned when it was deemed that the car would be too heavy and uncompetitive if it were equipped with a containment vessel strong enough to protect the driver from catastrophic flywheel failure. *Chrysler*

cars that were the purest expression of this think tank's capabilities were Patriot and CCV.

Introduced at the 1995 North American International Auto Show, Patriot revealed Castaing's ambition to win the 24 Hours of Le Mans in an unconventional way.

"I was trying to combine the idea of using speed and execution of racing to hone engineering skills and combine it with breakthrough technology and bring some international racing connection to Chrysler, all in one program," Castaing explains. "I suggested we do a race car that would use hybrid powertrain technology for the purpose of winning Le Mans. If you look back, that idea of

using alternative technologies isn't farfetched. Others have tried it before, like the Howmet turbine at Le Mans and the Cummins diesel at Indy."

But the Patriot was an electric hybrid unlike any ever seen before. A two-stage gas turbine engine fueled by liquefied natural gas powered the alternators that generated the current. And a flywheel spinning at 58,000 rpm stored energy to provide a boost for acceleration.

The chassis was built by Adrian Reynard, a successful race car constructor who built cars for use in CART, IMSA, and Le Mans. Built to meet the tight specifications of the Automobile Club d' Ouest (ACO), which sanctions the 24 Hour of Le Mans race, Patriot was an open-cockpit carbon fiber monocoque that weighed about 1,600 pounds.

The technology consisted of three main systems. The first was a 525-volt three-phase AC induction traction motor that weighed 143 pounds and was capable of turning at 24,000 rpm. The second was a water-cooled turbo-alternator, a two-stage gas turbine that turned at 50,000 rpm at low speed and 100,000 rpm at high speed that had a built-in three-phase alternator. That unit weighed 186 pounds. Finally, the 147-pound SatCon flywheel system used three-phase permanent magnets in a Halbach array to spin the vacuum-housed composite flywheel at 58,000 rpm.

"Instead of making it a reasonable hybrid, we stretched a bit too far by deciding to run it on liquefied natural gas to make the point that it was burning clean," Castaing recalls. "At the time, we were working on flywheels for passenger car applications so it was natural for us to look at the flywheel energy storage for the car. We were also interested in the advanced power controllers to run the hybrid electric powertrain, so all that made a lot of sense."

In fact, the development work on Patriot led to Chrysler taking out some patents on the technology. "If you remember, flywheels at that time were very much in favor as a way to store energy," Castaing says, noting that Chrysler was not alone in pursuing the technology. In fact,

A gas turbine engine mounted in the Patriot's sidepod provides the electrical power to spool up the flywheel. The fuel is liquified natural gas. *John Lamm*

the founders of Compaq computers, the Rosen brothers, had actually built a prototype flywheel hybrid electric of their own.

"We tried to make a super flywheel," Castaing says. "This one was huge because of its size and the amount of energy we need to accumulate for racing purposes. I realized through testing that running this machine with this much energy alongside a fuel tank could endanger the pilot. The containment vessel we would have needed to

capture that kind of energy was too big to take racing. We found out what the rest of the industry found out: flywheels were not practical for cars."

The Patriot that was shown at the North American International Auto Show was a runner "if you pushed it down a hill," Castaing laughs. Although a running prototype of the flywheel power unit was eventually built, it was determined during dyno testing, when there were two catastrophic failures of the flywheel, that the technology

CCV, which started life as the China Concept Vehicle and later became the Composite Concept Vehicle, looks just like the Citroen 2CV that provided its inspiration. The thermoplastic body is inexpensive to produce and could open new markets for automobiles in developing countries. *John Lamm*

too dangerous to put into a race car, let alone one fueled by a cryogenic fuel. The chassis developed by Reynard, however, hasn't gone to waste. A program using a conventional engine in an evolution of that chassis was announced for Le Mans 2000.

Even though other companies like Ferrari (which had introduced its own traditionally powered open-cockpit racers at the time) scoffed at the Chrysler effort, Castaing believes "the Patriot was wonderful. It was a real concept with so many facets to the idea. The car itself, the technology, the high-risk approach has to be admired. It was like building the SR-71, except that our car never flew."

The most significant of the Liberty cars, however, was CCV, a low cost, small vehicle designed for developing economies. CCV initially stood for China Concept Vehicle. In the mid-1990s, the Chinese government invited auto manufacturers from around the world to present proposals for a car that could put the populace on wheels. Most companies pitched ideas for building conventional five- or six-passenger sedans.

"It was obvious to some of us that once you have created a plan to give a Mercedes-Benz or a Buick [the eventual winners of the competition] to every senior bureaucrat in the government, there wasn't much of an auto industry in China beyond that," Castaing asserts. "Driving around in the countryside, you realize there's no way they can afford expensive cars. What the Chinese need is what the U.S. economy needed in the 1920s when Henry Ford created the Model T that every one of his employees could buy. It was a simple car that wasn't the most sophisticated, but it was solid, easy to maintain, and affordable."

Castaing challenged Moore's Liberty group to develop a car that was half the cost and half the weight of the Neon. He had in mind the kind of car his father had when Castaing was growing up in postwar France, a Citroen 2CV. "I told Tom we needed to develop the kind of car that people in the 1950s were looking for. I realized quickly that when I talked to Tom about the 1950s, he was

looking at the Chevrolet Bel Air, and I could tell by his eyes that we were not connecting."

So Castaing had the company acquire two cars, a Citroen 2CV and a Panhard PL17. The Panhard was an aluminum-bodied sedan powered by a 750 cc four-stroke motorcycle engine, similar to the type powering the 2CV.

"I said, forget the Panhard PL17—that was kind of the upscale car," Castaing said. "But the 2CV—Citroen produced millions and millions of them. I bet Tom if we were to analyze it, we would probably find it was half the weight and half the cost of Neon."

Castaing was right, but of course, such a car didn't offer the safety or the creature comforts of today's cars. The 2CV was basic bare-bones transportation designed for people who could afford one-and-a-half motorcycles.

But the 2CV did have some attributes that would come in handy even in modern times in a developing country. One of the hallmarks of the Citroen was its long suspension travel, so it was comfortable on unpaved roads. Also, the simplicity of such things as exposed hinges and flat-paned glass (which was simpler to make than curved glass) made a car like the 2CV much easier to manufacture, which again resulted in a low-cost vehicle affordable by the masses.

Castaing wasn't content merely to copy the original. He challenged Moore to develop a car that would use modern technology to meet the same weight and cost objectives, yet offer the kind of safety and creature comforts people have come to expect from automobiles.

The project began and the first concepts were called R2CV (for "our" 2CV) and later, China Concept Vehicle, which was CCV, both names obviously paying homage to Citroen.

The CCV was equipped with a Briggs & Stratton horizontally opposed, air-cooled, two-cylinder, four-stroke engine and a continuously variable transmission. Moore developed a long travel suspension strut that was actually less expensive than the original 2CV suspension. But the real breakthrough was the body of the car. It was made of plastic and would require no painting.

A Briggs & Stratton horizontally opposed, two-cylinder ohv engine provides power through a simple belt-driven CVT. *John Lamm*

"We wanted to have a new, low-investment process to make the car," Castaing says. "One year at the Frankfurt show, I was staying in Weisbaden and they have a model store across from the hotel. I was looking at buying a few models for my collection. On the way back on the company plane, I thought it would be neat if we could do a car like these models, because they are beautiful, very detailed. All we would have to do is just find a machine to blow the plastic or shoot the plastic in bigger parts to make a car."

Castaing met with Moore and told him to forget all the traditional approaches to composites because these processes, which usually involve layering resins, are slow and are not practical because of the time it takes make and

finish with paint. Castaing wanted to go with thermoplastics. "These are the high-volume inexpensive plastic pieces that we see every day like the case of your computer or the case of your phone," Castaing observes. "You can make beautiful shapes if it is done right. Tom went on this search for several weeks, looking for a press and injection molded pieces the size of a car."

It was the first time that the design of a car was literally found in a trash bin. Moore found two companies, one in France and the other near Grand Rapids, Michigan, which made plastic garbage dumpsters about the size of a small car.

"They were huge presses," Castaing recalls. "The process was to learn how to design a car in injection molded plastic, in an inexpensive material like PET [polyethylene terephthalate]. We had to learn how we would go about designing the car in pieces that could be molded. We found a way to do it in four major pieces that would be the two outside halves and the two inside halves. Then there would be a hood on the front, doors on the side, and a little trunk cover."

Moore had the company in Grand Rapids making molds and running presses, while Liberty teamed with a company in Canada and a couple of plastic suppliers to refine the process, do concept tools, and create the CCV.

Castaing believes thermoplastic is the next major step in car building. "If you look at the history of car bodies, it began with wood on wood, then it became steel on wood, then steel stamping on steel stamping, then steel monocoque (or unit body). Now we're trying to introduce injected-molded plastics on a subframe of steel. It is logical—the same way steel has replaced wood, plastic will replace steel. You look back at instrument panels of cars in the 1950s and they were steel. Now they are plastic. It was logical that we try to do something like that."

Castaing believes the CCV is the answer for developing countries. Other world cars competing in this niche, like the Fiat Palio, are less expensive than small cars selling in the industrialized world, but Castaing notes that these vehicles still use traditional methods, namely steel bodies that need to be stamped, welded, and painted. The CCV, on the other hand, merely needs PET and molding presses to produce the car, no welding shop or paint operation. "When you do a fully accounted cost of the car, it was much less expensive than any approach," Castaing says. But the car failed to win the competition. "When we went to China to present the car, it turned out to be a fiasco."

The problem was that no one believed in the car as fervently as Castaing. "It was presented by Midwestern Americans to bureaucrats in Beijing," Castaing says. "The people from the United States were not comfortable presenting a car that was not in their minds a real car, because it looked funny and used all this plastic, while the bureaucrats wanted to have a Mercedes-Benz.

"After having spent a lot of money for the presentation, everybody came back from there and was extremely upset about the way it went because we wasted a lot of money on this thing—the trip and all that," Castaing recalls. "But I knew that if you ask the bureaucrats they will want a Mercedes. When GM went there they asked for a Buick. The car of the future for China is a Buick?"

Castaing says: "Tom Gale was almost embarrassed that we presented the car because he thought it was not a styling statement that was on par with his reputation. I said to Tom that people will see what this car is about. He was all sick because the windows were flat. But it was essential to the design because when you go to this country, they can't make curved glass."

Castaing tried one more time with the car when he headed Chrysler's International Operations before his retirement. "I went back to China and instead of talking to people in Beijing, I suggested we do three or four cars and give them to farmers in the middle of nowhere for a month or two and see what happens." But Castaing believes that the car will never fly there because of the mindset of China's central planners.

This display showcases an automated fixture that could be used in gluing the four major body pieces of the CCV together, like a giant plastic model. Such inexpensive production techniques would keep the purchase price for the CCV low in developing countries. *Chrysler*

Still, the technology introduced by CCV, which by this time had been renamed the Chrysler Composite Concept Vehicle, lives. Injected-molded body panels, because of their low cost, were integral parts of such concepts as the Intrepid ESX II, the Pronto, and most recently, Pronto Spyder. One of the hurdles yet to be surmounted is whether the public is ready for a car with a matte finish and molded-in color. If scratch resistant, lightweight plastic cars that aren't shiny ever hit the road, you'll have Francois Castaing, and Liberty, to thank.

CHAPTER EIGHT

FUTURE STARS

At the 1995 North American International Auto Show, Chrysler wowed the press with what had become its traditional news conference stunt. This time it was the launch of the third generation minivan, which had the vehicle "leapfrogging the competition" by vaulting over cardigan-clad Bob Lutz and chairman Bob Eaton, who read a poem extolling the van's virtues.

That show was particularly significant because Ford began to strike back at Chrysler's ascendancy in both concept car and production car styling. Ford took the wraps off GT90, a V-12 two-seat sports car that had a Stealth fighter look to it, all angles and triangles, as well as the Lincoln L2K, a seemingly production-ready two-seat roadster. In reality, it wasn't a go, but the basic package provided the basis for the 2001 revival of the Thunderbird.

But far more important for Ford was the unveiling of the 1996 Taurus, nearly a year before its on-sale date. The Taurus, which established the aerodynamic look for the mass market, was the 1994 sales champ (*Automotive News*

reported Taurus sales of 387,037, compared to Chrysler's total of 288,533 for all LH models). Yet Ford's 1991 reskin had been considered too conservative when compared to the swoopy LH models.

Ford prided itself on design leadership and now found itself playing catch-up with lowly Chrysler and its cab forward LH cars. Ford vice president of design Jack Telnack decided that the next Taurus, despite its popularity in the market, had to convey the sort of breakthrough design of the original, and he unveiled a radical shape that took the "jellybean" look to new extremes. The new car, in addition to being soft and round, repeatedly emphasized an oval theme, from the headlights to the rear window and even on the dash, where the radio and heater controls were concentrated in an oval cluster.

Ford had taken a page from Chrysler's book about polarizing design. People either loved the new Taurus or hated it. As it would turn out, there would be more of the latter than the former. Part of the problem was that the

LHX, though much larger than the Chrysler LHS it foreshadows, accurately portrays the grille theme as well as the overall proportion of the new car. *John Lamm*

Eagle Jazz is the first indication that Chrysler is considering a shorter LH for export purposes. The styling is rounded, heavily influenced by the Porsche 911. *Chrysler*

exterior shape itself compromised interior functionality. The drooping rear end came at the sacrifice of trunk space; the fast angle on the rear window cut rear headroom and made it difficult to get in and out of the rear seats without hitting your head on the roof. Within four years, Ford would have a more conventionally styled replacement on the market with a traditionally shaped rectangular backlight, a tall trunk that gave the car a stronger, more wedge shape, and sharper-edge body panels.

"When we saw the Taurus, I thought it was great," Gale says, referring not to the design, but rather where Chrysler had put Ford strategically. "You can react by not doing enough, which is what some people will do. You can react by overdoing it or going too far. There must have

been a huge discussion at Ford, where they decided 'We're going to invent what's next.' "

Gale believes it was a huge miscalculation. Taurus was taking soft, round shapes to new extremes at a time when cars in general were softly shaped. "We all know," Gale explains, "that if everything is soft, the next thing you're going to do, you're going to put a crease on something. You're going to start tightening things up. It's just the way the world works."

At the same time, Gale and his design team were wrestling with what sort of direction to take with the next LH. Would they do a mild, evolutionary facelift or a radical redesign of the trend-setting sedans? At that 1995 show was a concept car that was virtually overlooked by the press corps. It was called the Eagle Jazz and it showed that Gale & Co. had no intention of backing off.

Chrysler would later kill the Eagle brand. But at the time, the LH family consisted of Intrepid and Concorde as the entry-level models at Dodge and Chrysler; the Eagle Vision was the sporty LH, while the New Yorker and LHS were the pure luxury models. Eagle Vision, with its taut suspension and clean styling, was badged a Chrysler for European export.

For the second generation, it was decided that the New Yorker would be dropped and that, in order to compete effectively in Europe, a "five-meter" model would be needed. Standard executive class cars in Europe rarely exceeded this measurement, which is nearly a half-foot shorter than the 201.6-inch overall length of the Vision.

The Eagle Jazz was the first indication that Chrysler would be building a five-meter car in its next generation LH. Though it rode on the standard 113-inch wheelbase of the LH, it was only 175.8 inches in overall length, or about 4.5 meters long. A hatchback, the Jazz had the look and feel of a sporty European sedan. Adding to that sportiness was a fully independent suspension that featured a modified double wishbone up front and a multilink rear. The transmission was Chrysler's sporty, sequentially shifted AutoStick automatic. Power came from a 2.5-liter V-6, making 175 horsepower. Though the LH models were powered by 3.3- and 3.5-liter V-6s, the smaller powerplant was considered a necessity for Europe with its high taxes on fuel and large displacement engines.

"The fact that it looked like a four-door 911 was not coincidental," Lutz observes. "That [Jazz] concept eventually evolved into the 300M." Though the shape of the Jazz was nothing like the 300M, it is the package that is important. It was a sign that Chrysler design was serious about pushing the envelope further on cab forward.

"Jazz took the cab forward, wheels-to-the-corner approach and extended the windshield even further over the front wheels," Neil Walling explains. "The driver-oriented interior was composed of functional shapes rather than flowy curvaceous lines, and there was a strong emphasis on ergonomics."

The Jazz also explored a unique approach to hatchback design. While Europeans embrace the practicality of hatches, Americans tend to want the security that a trunk provides. Beneath the hatch was a smaller trunk lid that sealed the passenger compartment from outside elements when the rear was open, a best-of-both-worlds approach.

The Eagle Jazz was almost a stealth concept, tipping the company's hand that it was considering a shorter LH with a more radical approach to cab forward, but at the same time revealing little about how these cars would actually look.

Jazz is a hatchback, but to appeal to more traditional American tastes, there is a second cover beneath the hatch, which acts like a conventional trunk lid. *John Lamm*

A conventional 3.5-liter V-6 is found beneath the LHX's unconventional clamshell hood. *John Lamm*

As work progressed on the next generation LHs, Gale insisted that each studio also work on a show car version. He was a big believer that the show cars, which were done after the basic design work was completed on the production versions, would set up a push-pull relationship in the studio. The designers could be more expressive on the show cars and would tend to do more aggressive shapes on details like the headlamps. These details in turn would be grafted back onto the production models. So while the concept cars were actually done last, they still had an impact on the real car's final detailing.

Chrysler came to the 1996 Detroit show with only two concepts, the Chrysler LHX and Intrepid ESX, literal interpretations of the next generation LH sedans that underscored the seriousness of this project.

The LHX and Intrepid ESX foreshadowed different aspects of the LH program. The Chrysler showed in broad strokes what the LHS would look like. But more important, the basic mechanical package was spot-on with the production car.

The concept car was oversized to make a grand gesture. It rode on a 124-inch wheelbase and was 214 inches in overall length. By contrast, the production LHS would have a 113-inch wheelbase and be only 207 inches long. The LHX was wide—77.9 inches—again nearly 3 inches wider than the production model. Even the wheel and tire package was massive, with 19-inch fronts and 20-inch rear tires. The engine was Chrysler's 3.5-liter V-6 with an estimated 250 horsepower (in production it would be 253). And it had the egg-crate grille that predicted the squarish shape of the production LHS opening.

The interior on the LHX experimented with graceful, simple forms that used wood accents and chrome "jewelry" for the door handles and a brushed aluminum look on some of the bezels surrounding the controls. The instruments were clustered in a single pod in the middle of the dashboard (which would make right-hand drive conversion simpler). There was a bona fide reason for the 124-inch-long wheelbase. Engineers constructed a cross-body bulkhead inside the car (almost a dual cowl approach) that housed an entertainment system and storage compartment for the rear seat passengers. The bulkhead not only provided a way to package amenities for the rear seat passen-

gers, but it also helped stiffen the overall structure and provided additional protection in side impacts.

The Intrepid ESX, on the other hand, had dimensions much closer to the production Intrepid and as a result, the overall design was similar to what you see on the road today. The ESX used the LH's 113-inch wheelbase and was 195 inches long (about a half foot shorter than the production model and about the size of the 300M). Again, the designers filled the wheel wells with 19-inch front and 20-inch rear rims.

The face of the ESX, with its slit-like lamps and Viper-like details, helped the designers push for a similarly aggressive look on the production Intrepid that would bow in 1998.

"When you look at LHX and Intrepid ESX, the graphics, the lamps, all those things came through to

More faithful to the overall dimensions of the Intrepid, ESX also accurately predicts the styling theme for Dodge's new family sedan. *John Lamm, Chrysler*

The wild interior says the ESX is a show car, after all. The center console has a contoured, almost organic sweep to it. *John Lamm*

Intrepid ESX is a hybrid, using a three-cylinder diesel to recharge the car's battery pack and assist with acceleration. *John Lamm*

production," Gale notes. "Unless we did that, I thought we were running a risk to put the concept cars out there and then hear people say the production cars aren't as good. I never heard that with the LHs. When we rolled out the production cars, people made the tie to the concept cars. Everybody embraced what had gone on and appreciated the fact that we had done those cars that way. It made the concept cars that much more meaningful. It was further evidence that concept cars really were part of the process."

But the ESX was far more than a literal interpretation of the next Intrepid. Francois Castaing marshaled the forces from Liberty to graft research work being conducted on the Partnership for a New Generation Vehicle (PNGV), a federal program designed to develop a proto-type family car of the future capable of delivering 80 miles per gallon.

"We thought, why not have a show car that is devoted to showing where we were on meeting our PNGV goals?" Castaing says.

The powertrain of the Intrepid ESX was a diesel/electric hybrid. A 1.8-liter three-cylinder diesel engine, which produced 75 horsepower, sat beneath the hood and was mated to a Kohler alternator. The output charged a battery pack with spiral-wound lead-acid batteries. Current drawn from the batteries, with an additional boost from the alternator as needed, powered two 125-horsepower Zytec electric motors, each one connected directly to a rear wheel. Four-wheel disc brakes provided additional regenerative battery charging when decelerating or stopping the car.

The problem with the hybrid powertrain, though, is that it was heavier than a conventional gasoline engine. As a result, the ESX became a test bed for alternatives to the traditional steel body. Though it had the dimensions of a full-size family sedan, the ESX, thanks to its intensive use of aluminum, tipped the scales at just 2,880 pounds, about 600 pounds less than a conventional steel unit body car.

Coinciding with the launch of the regular production Intrepid in 1998, an improved version of the concept car, called ESX2, was unveiled. This vehicle married the PET recyclable plastic of the Liberty-developed CCV to a drivetrain that relied primarily on a 1.5-liter three-cylinder diesel assisted by a battery-powered electric motor. That motor was used to run the accessories and provide additional boost for acceleration. Because it relied on the electric system as an assist rather than a primary means of motivation, Chrysler dubbed the ESX2 a "Mybrid," for mild hybrid.

The Mybrid had several advantages. Regenerative braking could be used to recharge the batteries, eliminating the need to plug in the vehicle at night. Also, the battery pack was smaller and lighter (only 130 pounds, versus 180 pounds in the original ESX), which also meant less cost ($4,000 versus $10,000). A smaller battery pack resulted in more cargo space, some 19.9 cubic feet versus 15 cubic feet in the ESX. The electrically assisted diesel engine was capable of delivering 70 miles per gallon, an improvement of 15 miles per gallon over ESX. This high fuel economy doesn't necessarily mean a lack of performance. Engineers said the car was capable of 0-60 miles per hour in 12 seconds and that 10 seconds was an attainable goal.

The high fuel economy was delivered by an electronically shifted five-speed manual transmission, which the driver treated just like an automatic. But because of the direct mechanical linkup with the engine, the five-speed improved overall fuel economy by eight miles per gallon.

The plastic body of the ESX2, which Chrysler claimed could be molded in three minutes, comprised six large pieces. It lowered vehicle curb weight by 500 pounds over the aluminum-bodied ESX. The cost savings were considerable—Chrysler estimated that the ESX2 would cost about $15,000 over the $25,000 sticker of a conventional Intrepid. That compared to the original ESX, which because of its aluminum body and more exotic hybrid drivetrain would have cost $95,000.

The plastic body of the ESX2, with its blunter nose, large wheels with flat covers, and rear skirts, had a drag

ESX2 trades an aluminum body for a lighter plastic one and incorporates such wind-cheating devices as rear wheel skirts, solid wheel discs, and various aerodynamic aids that deploy at speed. *John Lamm*

coefficient of 0.19 compared to 0.25 for the previous concept car. In addition to the slicker body shape, aerodynamics were improved with the help of rocker panels that lowered at speed, a deployable rear spoiler, and a windscreen that lowered from behind the grille.

Though the basic shape of the Intrepid ESX2 was old news by the time it was launched in 1998, it foreshadowed the next big step in Chrysler's evolution of its concept car strategy. Chrysler's entire 1999 crop of show cars would combine bold styling statements with alternative fuel technology just like the ESX2. They would become concepts with a conscience.

CHAPTER NINE

CONCEPTS WITH A CONSCIENCE

The use of concept cars to showcase new power-train technology was nothing new for Chrysler as it prepared itself for the 1999 North American International Auto Show. Eight years earlier, the Neon concept featured two-stroke engine technology while the 1992 Epic was an electric.

In 1999, however, it was decided the company would go all the way. Every concept vehicle would highlight some sort of alternative propulsion. It would be a powerful message that cars can be fun and at the same time socially responsible.

There would be the Dodge Charger R/T, a modern-day interpretation of the hairy muscle cars of the late 1960s and early 1970s. But instead of being a gas-guzzling behemoth, this new-age asphalt burner would inhale compressed natural gas.

The Dodge Power Wagon, a brute of a pickup that recalled the hardy full-size Dodge pickups of postwar America, would be a diesel that would rewrite the notion that these engines, though efficient, spew soot everywhere. The Power Wagon would run on a new synthetic fuel that actually burned cleaner than gasoline.

Capitalizing on the ever-larger sport-ute craze, the Jeep Commander would be a Hummer-size vehicle, and yet it would tread lightly with the use of fuel-cell technology.

And finally, the Chrysler Citadel would probe the feasibility of Chrysler jumping into the so-called crossover vehicle market, those hybrid car/SUV luxury liners. But the Citadel would do it with a twist—it would be called a hybrid-hybrid because it would offer the power of a V-8 by using the 3.5-liter V-6 with an electric motor assist.

"You look at the Charger using CNG, or the Power Wagon diesel, the Citadel being a different kind of hybrid, or the Commander," Gale observes. "All across the board we were sending a message not just about our future products, but our future technology."

Bob Lutz believes marrying high technology and concepts is smart business. "You do that for two reasons. First

As a lifelong Chrysler designer, Tom Gale understands the company's heritage as evidenced by his modern interpretation of the Charger. Proportions of the show car and the late 1960s Charger are remarkably similar, although certain cues, like the front grille treatment, differ. *John Lamm*

For the 1999 auto show circuit, all of Chrysler's concepts sported alternative powerplants. They are, clockwise from left, Chrysler Citadel, Jeep Commander, Dodge Power Wagon, and Dodge Charger. *Bill Delaney*

you are genuinely exploring those technologies. The second reason, well, if you were to show a Chrysler 300 concept today with an 8.0-liter V-10 and 450 horsepower, you would be acting as a lightning rod for the environmentally aware side of the press corps and you would likely be vilified."

Gale is particularly proud of the Jeep Commander, a member of a class of vehicles—large SUVs—that have come under intense fire for being socially irresponsible.

"What a surprise," Gale says. "Everyone thought our fuel cell concept would be some sort of swoopy egg shape and it appears in a straight-up, big sport-utility. Well why not? It's just enough to take a bite out of those so anxious to be down on the industry. It kept them thinking and off-guard."

While Gale is proud of the statement the Commander makes, it's the CNG Charger R/T that is closest to his heart. As an owner of a 1970 AAR 'Cuda, Gale has long championed the idea of a modern-day muscle car, going back to the Venom in 1995.

Heading up the team developing Charger and the Citadel was Neil Walling, vice president of advanced design.

"We had the opportunity to pay homage to a classic design from our past while updating for the future," Walling says of the Charger exercise. The biggest change from the original was the decision to go with four instead of two doors. "We originally sketched it with two doors, but the more we looked at it, we couldn't ignore the opportunity it presented for four doors," Walling notes. Contributing to that change was the fact that the two-door car market had been shrinking, precisely because sedans were becoming better looking.

The Charger was a unique study in that it blended styling cues from the past and dimensions and characteristics from Dodge's current product line-up. The "Coke-bottle" shape of the late 1960s Charger R/T was reproduced with styling elements consistent with the Viper-inspired Dodge family.

"It has muscular lines that are more exaggerated because of the package, with big offset shoulders over the rear wheels," says Joe Dehner, who was responsible for exterior design. "This Charger R/T has a menacing look to the front end, low and wide with a powerful-looking rear end. Some aspects remind me of the Viper." Those touches included the cross-hair split grille opening, the functional side scoops, and the chrome-plated centrally mounted exhaust.

"The original Charger had two nonfunctional scoops stamped into its hood, whereas we have one real scoop at the leading edge of the hood, closest to the front grille," Dehner points out. "The early sketches had that distinctive Charger grille, as if the car swallowed a very wide harmonica. We even played around with the bumblebee stripe around the rear end. But we went away from that to a more modern, fresher statement.

Charger is a blend of new and old styling cues, from the Intrepid to the Coke-bottle-shaped Charger of the late 1960s. *Chrysler*

The Charger's interior mixes modern carbon fiber accents with retro-looking gauges and an updated version of the pistol grip shifter. *Chrysler, Bill Delaney*

Even though the Charger's 4.7-liter makes 325 horsepower, it's a good corporate citizen by burning clean natural gas. *Chrysler*

Even the signature flying buttress [C-pillar] resembles today's Intrepid more than the original Charger."

While the Charger R/T design shared the same long nose and rearward cab of its namesake, the dimensions were much more compact. At 187 inches in overall length, it was considerably shorter than the 203-inch-long original. And it weighed 650 pounds less, with a curb weight of 3,000 pounds.

The interior of the Charger R/T was an interesting blend of retro touches with modern machine-age design.

The five-speed manual had a "pistol grip" shifter reminiscent of 1970s Mopar muscle cars. The doors and lower part of the center console were body-colored metal, while the transmission hump had matte-finished carbon fiber, which has the feel of a stripped-down street racer. Another retro touch was the drilled aluminum pedals. The molded seats, fat steering wheel with aluminum-finish spokes, as well as the instrument bezels and controls for the radio and air conditioning, were created with a more modern edge to them.

Dodge Power Wagon has a cab similar in size to the Dakota, yet projects a macho image that is larger than life, or at least certainly larger than a full-size Ram 4x4. *Chrysler*

Beneath the hood sat a modified version of the 4.7-liter V-8 used in the Jeep Grand Cherokee that produced a healthy 325 horsepower. The CNG-fueled engine enabled the Charger R/T to meet California's stringent Ultra Low Emission Vehicle (ULEV) regulations.

The key to making the conversion work was a light-weight rear tank system, which provided up to 300 miles of range without a significant weight penalty or sacrifice of trunk space. These three cylinders were used to store compressed natural gas at 3,600 psi and had lightweight outer shells made of carbon fiber and fiberglass strands wound in an epoxy resin. The cylinders were lined with gas-impermeable High Density Polyurethane thermosplastic. The entire tank array was encased in a foam egg-crate carrier to absorb impacts.

DODGE POWER WAGON

When Dodge decided to become a serious player in the pickup market, it turned to semi tractors as an

The Power Wagon combines the utility of a work truck with the upscale image of a high-style luxury vehicle. *Bill Delaney*

inspiration for its tough Ram truck and carved out its own unique niche.

And as the pickup market grew, it attracted a new following of people who discovered that these vehicles were not just for work. Instead, customers were looking to trucks to make the same kind of statement a luxury car would make.

Chrysler heard these people and decided that if it did a luxury truck, it would not only play on that tough truck theme, but it would also reach back into its heritage to play off the Power Wagon.

The new Power Wagon certainly had the purposeful look of the original. With its full-fendered front end, large cross-hatch grille, and running boards, the Power Wagon evoked the imagery of a late 1940s truck and, yet, was modern. Although Lutz had little to do with the Power Wagon, he thinks it is one of the best concept vehicles ever executed by Chrysler. "I don't know a single pickup owner who wouldn't kill to own a truck like that."

The Power Wagon's 7.2-liter direct-injection Caterpillar inline six, which produced 780 ft-lb of torque, could certainly do the work of its namesake and then some. But the Power Wagon's purpose was twofold: to appeal to upscale buyers who wanted the ultimate truck and to prove that diesels need not be environmental pariahs.

"Our objective was to create more of a 'Sharper Image' truck than an everyday work truck," says Trevor Creed. "With this concept, we were asking, 'Is there room in the truck market to appeal to new customers who desire all the extras and still want the traditional capability of a truck to pull their boat and haul stuff?' "

While the styling evoked the ruggedness of the original Power Wagon, this concept was anything but the hardy work truck of postwar America. For one thing, it was much larger. Standing on huge 35-inch tires, the Power Wagon, at 77 inches tall, towered 4 inches above the 4x4 Ram pickup. The basic chassis was from the Ram, but the cabin was more the size of the Dodge Dakota, giving the truck a closely coupled cab similar in layout to the original Power Wagon.

Even though the shape was somewhat retro because of the running boards, round head and taillamps, vented hood, and separate fenders, the Power Wagon was thoroughly modern in features. It had rear-hinged access doors to get at the storage space behind the front seats and a power rear liftgate.

"Early in the design process, we debated whether to do a basic work truck versus an upscale truck," says Mark Allen, the Power Wagon's exterior designer. "We chose to distance ourselves from the ultimate simplicity of the original truck. That's why you don't see the spare tire mounted on the side of the truck box or free-standing headlamps. I see this as a thrill-seeker's truck, for the gear-oriented sports enthusiast. It's a vehicle to take you rock climbing or mountain biking."

Commander has seating for five in individual bucket seats front and rear. Wood accents, leather seating material, and aluminum fascias give Commander a luxurious, high-tech aura. *Chrysler*

The Power Wagon is not just a heavy lifter. The interior, with its cognac-colored leather and ash wood accents, has a luxurious, upscale look. *Chrysler*

While the purpose of this truck was playful, that doesn't mean functionality had to suffer. The front of the vehicle was equipped with an integrated winch capable of pulling an 18-wheeler out of a ditch. Gas-discharge projector beam headlamps provided excellent illumination. The tall ride height had great ground clearance for off-road operation of the 4x4 vehicle.

The all-work nature of the components was offset by the upscale design of the cabin. But interior designer Steve Sowinski couldn't use the original as much of an inspiration for the concept. The original Power Wagon's "deluxe cab" options included items like an armrest, sun visor, and dome light.

"People will have to stretch their imaginations to find similarities between the interior of this Power Wagon and the 1946 original. Whereas the original was a study in raw steel, we used a mix of new materials to get a clean, high-tech look," Sowinski explains.

The Commander looks as rugged as any full-size SUV on the market, but beneath its hood beats an eco-friendly fuel cell.
Bill Delaney

Commander wears the rugged good looks that are expected of all Jeeps. This Hummer-sized sport-ute could go into production, but with a conventional gasoline engine powerplant. Bill Delaney

The truck box and interior load floor behind the front seats were finished in European ash. It was decided to make the Power Wagon a two-seater and use the space at the rear of the cabin for storage only. The distressed leather and stainless steel finish on the door handles, shift levers, and steering wheel gave the interior the look of high-end furniture. The instruments were clustered in a single round binnacle, while the air conditioning system was controlled by three large knobs in the center of the dash, which gave the cockpit a clean, uncluttered look, reminiscent of the original Power Wagon's spartan interior.

The size of the Power Wagon belied its environmental friendliness. The engine motivating this monster was run on a new grade of fuel that promised to make diesels the engine of the future, not the past. Although diesels had a reputation for spewing soot into the atmosphere, the engines showed greater promise than gasoline engines because they were up to 40 percent more efficient in fuel economy. Better fuel economy translated to less carbon dioxide, which meant that diesels could be a great aid in meeting government restrictions on so-called greenhouse emissions.

"While we're not claiming to have already developed the perfect diesel engine, we are claiming that diesels have a significant future in the passenger car and truck industry," says Bernard Robertson, Chrysler's senior vice president of engineering technologies. "With further refinement of engine technologies, exhaust after-treatments and cleaner fuels, diesel engines will be a major player as we continue to look for more efficient and cleaner powertrain alternatives."

The Dodge Power Wagon ran on a synthetic fuel developed by a company called Syntroleum. This fuel, derived from abundant natural gas, had no sulfur or other agents that produce soot when burned.

Gale says in light of the regulatory crackdown on diesels, the purpose of the Power Wagon "was to send a message to the EPA that there is room for diesels in the fleet."

JEEP COMMANDER

A fuel cell is an environmentalist's dream. It uses hydrogen to produce electricity. The "exhaust" is water. The problem with fuel cell technology, however, is packaging. Hydrogen as a fuel is difficult to store; as a compressed gas, it takes up a lot of space. Liquid hydrogen will fit in a smaller space and give more range. Unfortunately, in its cryogenic state, it's difficult to handle and dangerous to the human touch.

Another solution is to convert an existing fuel, like gasoline or methanol, to hydrogen on board a vehicle, sort of like carrying your own refinery with you. Chrysler had announced that it was working on such a system to reform gasoline to hydrogen for use in a fuel cell. The benefits are twofold: you get the clean power aspects of the fuel cell

YES, THEY CAN BE DRIVEN

Tom Gale's edict that Chrysler's concepts be driveable is no joke. On a warm summer afternoon, I was invited to drive three of the company's 1999 concept cars, the Dodge Charger, the Dodge Power Wagon, and the Chrysler Citadel, at a small handling track behind the Daimler-Chrysler headquarters facility in Auburn Hills, Michigan.

Driving a million-dollar prototype is intimidating. Who wants to be known as the person who wrecked or broke a one-of-a-kind dream car? Show cars in general are not up to production standards, so I'm inclined to overlook the kinds of squeaks, rattles, and even driveability that I would take issue with in a production car.

"With the show cars, people are willing to cut you a lot of slack," Gale says. "I don't recall one where we have really gotten hammered. It's a little bit like hot rods. There's this kind of courtesy. You know that this is one man's expression. I think we get a little bit of that with show cars."

Still, it's one thing to see a concept rotating on a turntable, quite another to watch or actually drive it down the road. When I slid behind the seat of the Charger, I felt a certain sense of déjà vu mixed with the new. The pistol grip shifter felt familiar, as did the hefty clutch, which took some effort to push in as I twisted the key. The volatile CNG mix fed into the engine and made it spring to life instantly—which is unlike the old days, where it would take a few cranks to coax the car to life. And yet, the exhaust note was downright snarly, thanks to the free-flowing Borla tailpipes. A side benefit to using CNG is its clean burning properties, which allowed the Charger R/T to do its thing without a sound-deadening catalytic converter.

I selected a gear, dumped the clutch, and the Charger launched like a muscle car of yore. But the big surprise came quickly in the first corner — the Charger R/T actually liked to turn in. The meaty 19-inch front alloy wheels shod with P245/45R-19 rubber and the monster 20-inch rear wheels, which wore P295/40R-20 skins, along with Viper suspension bits were responsible for this agility. It got even better. After launching up about 100 miles per hour on the backstraight, the satisfying rush to speed was complemented by an equally satisfying and confidence-inspiring braking system, also adapted from the Dodge Viper. The brakes employed four-pot front calipers to keep the Charger R/T in check.

I found the power-assisted steering more up-to-date than retro. Rather than the over-boosted, light-effort steering I remember from my youth, the new age Charger had some heft as well as excellent on-center feel. Though the chassis still felt as if it needed a bit of sorting, I concluded that a rear-drive platform like this would be a welcome addition to the Dodge fleet.

Following my short romp in the Charger R/T, I did one last walk around. I noticed that the rear doors did nothing to detract from the car's sensuous shape. I could easily slip into the back seat. If I'd only had a car like this 30 years ago, there would have been fewer calls for "shotgun."

After that blast from the past in the Charger, the Dodge Power Wagon was a totally different proposition. Whereas the Charger promised brute off-the-line force, the Power Wagon's charm was found in its massive torque and a four-wheel drive system with the ability, it seemed, to climb walls.

The Power Wagon was the kind of diesel a soccer mom could love. With 780 lb-ft of torque on tap (and about 250 horsepower) from its Caterpillar six-cylinder diesel, the Power Wagon was quite tractable and easy to drive at low speeds. I could feel the massive amount of torque as it worked its way through the all-wheel-drive system down to the pavement.

The small cabin had the feel of a closely coupled sports car, albeit one that's flying at about 50 feet. The view out the windows of the Power Wagon was command-ing. It's the closest thing I've ever experienced to driving a monster truck.

I stood by the rear of the Power Wagon while it was running and noticed that there was no visible exhaust. And for a diesel with 7.2 liters of displacement, it was no noisier than the Cummins diesel offered as an option on the Ram 4x4. The Power Wagon proved to be such a crowd-pleaser on the show circuit that a production version will likely be tooled up sometime in the not too distant future.

While the Dodge Power Wagon projected this go anywhere, do anything attitude, the Citadel was more down to earth, but no less an impressive performer. Even though it was a hybrid, the Citadel felt very much like a conventional automobile, and a very luxurious one at that. The seats were soft and cushy, and the interior reminded me of the ultra-swank Chronos with its handsome instruments and tastefully appointed interior.

The electric motor provided its boost seamlessly, giving the V-6 the kind of pulling power you'd expect from a V-8, though I noted a bit of gear and electric motor noise that wouldn't pass muster in a production car.

I found that the Citadel started and drove like a conventional automobile. You never have to recharge the batteries, so there weren't any external plugs or other apparatus to indicate that this vehicle was part electric.

The gated shifter moved just like a normal automatic transmission lever into drive, and off I went. The car felt remarkably similar in dynamics to the 300M, with which it shares its platform and V-6 engine. The ride wasn't quite as cushy though, because of the huge show car wheels, P235/55R-19 tires front and P245/55R20 rubber in the rear.

The all-wheel-drive system provided excellent acceleration and promised surefootedness in bad weather. After a short stint behind the wheel of the Citadel, I was convinced that the combination of an electric power assist to conventional gas engines was an idea whose time may have come.

Citadel is a crossover vehicle, combining the styling of a car with the ride height and carrying capacity of a sport-utility vehicle. *Chrysler*

while, at the same time, you don't have to make any changes in the existing gasoline-based supply infrastructure.

But what you need is a vehicle with some size. As a result, Chrysler combined environmentalists' dream — a fuel cell — with their worst nightmare — a full-size SUV — in the Jeep Commander.

"This concept married the industry's most advanced powertrains with one of the fastest-growing market segments," says Creed. "With fuel cell technology under the hood, this vehicle took Jeep's pledge to 'Tread Lightly' on the environment very seriously."

It's a brute of a sport-ute. The Jeep Commander had Hummer-like proportions. It was 80 inches wide and stood 69.4 inches tall. The Commander had an aggres-

sive front end that incorporated the seven grille slats of the Grand Cherokee and flanked it with projector beam headlamps topped by amber turn signals. The projector beam headlights themselves were styled to resemble the intakes on jet engines.

"Commander has a machined, high-tech feel," says Steve Won, the vehicle's exterior designer. "Bauhaus design philosophy led me to the very clean, precise, and mechanical appearance."

Huge five-spoke wheels and an adjustable suspension that could add four inches to ride height and improve ground clearance gave an air of invincibility to the Commander. Though the Commander looked big and heavy, most of its weight came from the fuel cell

Citadel's tasteful interior looks as if its been lifted directly from Chrysler's line of LH sedans. *Chrysler*

and its fuel reformer, which weighed over 2,000 pounds. And yet, the overall weight of the Commander was about 5,000 pounds. How did they do that? They borrowed the concept of using a body made of recycled plastic soda pop bottles from the Pronto Spyder two-seater concept. The process reduced body weight by 50 percent and was 10 to 20 percent cheaper to produce than conventional steel panels. Designers envisioned using that technology to reduce body mass in order to accommodate the additional weight of the powerplant. For show purposes, the Commander was actually built of carbon fiber to simulate the weight savings of the new PET plastic body structure.

While the Commander was massive, engineers worked hard to improve the vehicle's aerodynamics. At highway speeds a spoiler deployed from the roof. The roof rack was integrated into the body structure to be raised only when needed. An underbelly pan smoothed the air flow beneath the vehicle and a heat exchanging panel on the cowl not only reduced drag but drew hot air out from the engine compartment to cool the fuel cell while it was in operation. Power from that fuel cell was fed to two

The Citadel's huge wheels and tires, aggressive nose, and a delicately designed greenhouse combines SUV ruggedness with the stylish good looks of a wagon. Bill Delaney

motors, one each for the front and rear axles to provide all-wheel drive.

Other functional bits on the outside of the Commander included a tow hitch cover that folded down to provide a step to access the roof, while the side view mirrors were equipped with wipers and convex glass to eliminate blind spots.

The high-tech aspects of the Commander were not limited to the drivetrain. Inside, a small laptop computer docked into the center console and provided GPS data and Internet access for real-time weather, traffic, and navigation as well as phone and e-mail communication. The computer could also be used for vehicle diagnostic information. A small microphone in the steering wheel allowed for hand-free cell calls as well as voice activation of the computer to send e-mail.

The 80-inch width provided for an extra-large center console and three-across bucket seating in the rear. The interior was upholstered in navy blue and contrasting cognac leather trim.

The fuel cell is still a distant dream. We may not see the technology on road-going vehicles before 2005. But the Commander itself was such a well-thought-out design that it could be equipped with a 4.7-liter V-8 or even the V-10 from the Viper and hit the roads to do battle with GM's Suburban and Ford's Excursion.

CHRYSLER CITADEL

You can call it a hybrid squared. The Chrysler Citadel was a blend of station wagon and sport-utility, and while the latter connotes all-wheel-drive capability, here's where the hybrid was squared. The four wheels were driven by two different propulsion systems: a 253-horsepower 3.5-liter V-6 powered the rear wheels in a conventional way, while a 70-horsepower electric motor handled the duties at the front.

"This is a new breed of crossover vehicle in a category all by itself," explains Walling. "It provides the driving passion of the Chrysler 300M with ample cargo room."

The idea was to offer V-8 levels of performance with V-6 fuel economy and emissions. An advanced engine control system tapped into the hybrid electric's lead-acid batteries for an extra boost to enhance both off-the-line acceleration and midrange passing. When the electric engine was not running, the turning motion of the front wheels and regenerative braking were recharging its batteries. The batteries were kept in a constant state of charge, somewhere between 40-60 percent of capacity, and never had to be plugged in to be recharged.

The Citadel had a bold egg-crate grille topped by the winged Chrysler logo. Sport-ute cues were imparted with the round driving lights and skid-plate accenting the front fascia. Large, six-spoke wheels, 19-inch front and 20-inch rear, are fitted with Goodyear Extended Mobility tires that would look equally appropriate on a Dodge Durango. While the lower half of the body was wide and muscular, the wagon-like greenhouse had more delicately drawn features that gave the Citadel an air of elegance. It's as if ItalDesign's Giorgetto Giugiaro and not Osamu Shikado, who also designed the 1998 Chrysler Chronos, penned the gentle upsweep of the glass area.

"Both cars (Citadel and Chronos) have heroic proportions," Shikado explains, "but they are very different statements. The Citadel is very contemporary, whereas the Chronos was the epitome of Chrysler heritage. The Citadel's windows, side panels, and tires are flush to a create a body section that designers call monocoque."

While the front doors opened conventionally, the power rear doors slid rearward making the vehicle accessible for wheelchair-bound motorists. Based on Chrysler's new LH platform, the Citadel had a much longer wheelbase (131 inches), stood 3 inches taller, and had 2 more inches of ground clearance than the Concorde sedan. The Citadel offered 20 cubic feet of storage room, only 2.2 cubic feet less than a Plymouth Voyager minivan.

The interior used leather similar to that found in premium luggage lines like Louis Vuitton and Coach. The silver-backed instrument cluster had a chronograph appearance, and ample swaths of brushed aluminum offset the matte black instrument panel binnacle and the lighter leather-covered surfaces. Interior designer Akino Tsuchiya wanted to create the feeling of a European luxury sedan with just a hint of Art Deco influence.

"I was able to keep the serious business look, yet add more character to it," she says. "That's most evident in the shape of the center vents, center console, radio stalks, steering wheel, and seats." The use of traditional wood, black jade leather, brushed aluminum, and chrome accents gave the Citadel's cockpit an aura of elegance.

A Chrysler-branded version of the Citadel, code-named CS, is in the works, though it uses traditional front-hinged rear doors. Unlike the show car, however, it will use a conventional gasoline engine to drive all four wheels.

Still, the impact of all these concepts, with their exploration of alternative technologies, indicates that dream cars will continue to play off green themes.

CHAPTER TEN

FROM CONCEPT TO REALITY

Perhaps Chrysler's single greatest contribution to the automotive industry from the decade of the 1990s was the company's approach to integrating show cars into the vehicle development process.

While it's true that the industry has a long history of occasionally producing concept cars, they were usually isolated instances rather than regular practice.

By using show cars to lift a brand's image, to condition the public to future styling trends, or to seek out new niches where none existed before, Chrysler has transformed concepts from mere eye candy to a valuable development tool, a philosophy to which virtually all manufacturers now subscribe.

The best demonstration of this philosophy in action is the development of the PT Cruiser, a vehicle that was literally shaped in public with a series of concepts, culminating with an industry first—the simultaneous launch of a show car and its production version. Along the way, each of the concepts had a specific task. The 1997 Plymouth Pronto explored a new niche. The Pronto Cruizer telegraphed the styling theme but also, as a three-door, tried to misdirect the competition. The 1999 PT Cruiser show car faithfully mirrored the 2001 production version, the PT Cruiser. And finally, the GT Cruiser offered a glimpse of what to expect after the vehicle, was launched.

Characterized as a "segment-buster" by Chrysler chairman Bob Eaton, the PT Cruiser was designed to appeal to a wide range of small car buyers by offering a high level of utility in an economical package that stood out from anything else on the road.

The seed was planted for the PT Cruiser in 1997 with the Pronto, a five-door "tall-car" concept. The Pronto was designed with two objectives in mind: the first, to explore the idea of a small car that could offer the utility of a minivan, and second, to again experiment with the low-cost plastic body panels first shown on the CCV.

In Europe, small minivans traditionally sell well, with Renault's Megane Scenic generally recognized as the

The finished Pronto Cruizer debuts at the Geneva Auto Show in March 1998. The vehicle is touted as merely a showcase for the company's 1.6-liter four-cylinder engine being jointly developed with BMW. *Chrysler*

Initial sketches of the Pronto show car envision a modern tall-car to compete with small European minivans. The folding canvas roof is a recurring Chrysler styling theme. *Chrysler*

breakthrough vehicle in the segment. It combined handsome styling with a high level of utility with seats that could flip, fold, or be removed altogether.

But small vans similar to the Scenic flopped in the United States. Nissan tried selling the Axxess, and Mitsubishi sold the Expo and Expo LRV (also badged Summits and sold by Chrysler as Eagle products). No matter how useful these small boxes on wheels were, they just couldn't capture the imagination of American car buyers.

"We kept exploring the concept," Lutz recalled, "but anytime you did a small minivan, no matter how much you disguised it, the American public would say, 'Yeah, interesting interior, right, um, yes. Thank you very much,' and move on." To Lutz, minivans carried the stigma of "mom-mobile." That stigma helped fuel the sales of sport-utilities, which offered the seating capacity of a minivan or station wagon yet projected a rugged, independent image.

Still, the idea of doing a tall vehicle off the Neon platform, particularly with Europe in mind, propelled the Pronto project forward.

Pronto's design was modern with just a few retro cues, such as the tall grille opening that echoed Prowler, the roll-back canvas sun roof, and the free-standing bumpers. Pronto had a 101-inch wheelbase and at 148.8 inches in overall length, was about 2 feet shorter than the Neon. Yet at 58 inches tall, it was 2 inches taller.

The interior, which featured front buckets and a rear, split fold-down bench, was roomy, practical, and flexible. The instruments were clustered in a single pod in the center of the dash, which accommodated either left- or right-hand drive. The engine was taken from the Neon, a 2.0-liter sohc four that made 132 horsepower. A three-speed automatic transaxle drove the front wheels. Typical of show cars, the wheel wells were filled with 18-inch alloy rims shod with P185/50R-18 tires. And the body was made of metal painted a matte finish to simulate composite body skins.

The Pronto Concept called for use of Acrylonitrile/Styrene/Acrylate (ASA) plastic with a single molded-in color that would eliminate the painting process and simplify assembly. In addition to the blow-molded bumpers, the Pronto was envisioned as offering two different color plastic trim options that would be compatible with the interior.

When the Pronto was launched, it received a much more enthusiastic response from the European press than American journalists. Despite the cool reception at home, the Pronto was significant because of its groundbreaking approach to small car proportions. The high roof allowed for a more upright passenger seating position, giving the driver the same command-of-the-road seating position found in SUVs and minivans. Until then, it was believed that as people shifted to SUVs, vans, and trucks, small cars would decline in popularity because people couldn't see around the larger vehicles and didn't feel safe. The answer is to make small cars not necessarily bigger, but taller. The

Interior sketch shows center-mounted instrumentation, another cost-saving move enabling the vehicle to be built in right- or left-hand drive configurations. *Chrysler*

drivers and passengers get better visibility and don't feel as intimidated by other vehicles on the road.

"Because of its technology and proportional possibilities, Plymouth Pronto represents a paradigm-breaking method of changing transportation as we know it," says Neil Walling. "Pronto gives people space where they need space and economy where they need economy."

With the upcoming change in the 2000 Neon, Gale says a decision was made to pursue the Pronto concept.

"We could have done the replacement Neon four-door and two-door," Gale recalls. "But we said, 'No, we've got two bullets to spend. We can't walk away from the four-door. But, okay, let's take the other one and do

The Pronto show car, which has a metal body, is painted in a matte finish to simulate a thermoplastic skin. While the architecture is new, retro cues like the Prowler stand-up grille and small bumpers add personality to Pronto. *Chrysler*

something different that people are going to pay money for. Everyone else is slugging it out trying to do passenger cars and we let others do that, while we go over here and do something else.'"

Getting to somewhere else, however, proved to be difficult. The design community in Chrysler was split over doing a modern looking vehicle closer to the Pronto concept or going retro.

Big proponents of going retro with PT Cruiser included Lutz; Chris Theodore, who headed up Neon platform development; Jim Holden, who was in charge of marketing; and Francois Castaing.

"Every time we had the PT Cruiser discussion, we were back to a look that was similar to the VW Golf, but slightly higher," Lutz says. But the designers had hit a wall and had a difficult time with the right shape for the car.

Finally, a design from Bryan Nesbitt, who at 27, was just two years out of Art Center College of Design, hit the right retro theme for the PT Cruiser.

"Things didn't happen until we started doing this funky retro-style body with the free-standing fenders," Lutz explains. "It's amazing nowadays how the free-standing fender theme works. It touches a nostalgia nerve you can't

The European press loved the shape and utility of Pronto, while in market research clinics, Americans worried that such a large glass hatch would invite theft. *Chrysler*

reach in any other way. Think of the Atlantic, think of the Prowler, think of the Ram pickup, and think of the PT Cruiser. It's all getting away from the laid-on-its-side-cereal-box look and getting back to hoods, fenders, and decks. It is not shameful to look at the past."

The retro theme worked on two levels: it hit the nostalgia button, and it also conveyed the idea that this was a uniquely American product.

That was crucial as the project headed into its second phase with the Pronto Cruizer. As work progressed on the PT44, Chrysler decided to try out the retro styling theme

on the public. It was thought that the hot rod look would work in America, since the modern approach to these types of vehicles had failed. The key would be Europe, which liked the modern style found in Renault's Scenic. If Europeans warmed to a retro version, it would confirm that retro would be the way to go, since the plan was to sell PT Cruiser globally.

A concept car was commissioned for the 1998 Geneva Motor Show, and it would mark only the second time that a Chrysler show car had debuted in Europe, the first being the Portofino at Frankfurt more than a decade earlier. The

In an effort to see if a retro look would have legs in Europe, a three-door version of the Pronto, called the Pronto Cruizer, is sketched by designer Bryan Nesbitt. The rear end is steeply raked and aggressively gestured. *Chrysler*

designers decided to make the Pronto Cruizer a three-door, even though the PT44 was being developed as a five-door.

Part of the Pronto Cruizer's brief, according to Neil Walling, was "a showcase for our joint venture engine with BMW, a 1.6-liter four cylinder." BMW and Chrysler had an arrangement to build that 115-horsepower engine along with a 1.4-liter unit in South America for use primarily in European markets.

The Pronto Cruizer could be viewed as Chrysler's answer to the New Beetle. It offered styling cues that were uniquely American with the kind of features that Europeans had come to expect from cars in this class. In other words, rather than offering yet another interpretation of the Renault Megane Scenic, Chrysler served up a heaping helping of American culture.

"American design has some interesting roots," Walling says, referring to the history of the hot rod. "Some of it was bad, some of it was really bad. But a lot of it was good. This Cruizer could only come from our culture."

The Pronto Cruizer, unlike the plastic-body Pronto proposal, was intended from the start as a steel unit-body vehicle. It rode on the Neon's 104-inch platform, but at 167.2 inches was nearly 5 inches shorter. It was also 4 inches taller. Again, as a concept car, it had an aggressive wheel and tire package: the fronts were 18x7-inch wheels with P205/55R-18 tires, while the rear were 19x7.5-inch rims with P215/55R-19 rubber.

The huge four-wheel disc brakes were taken from the Viper, while the MacPherson strut suspension at all four corners and the five-speed manual transmission came directly from the Neon.

Nesbitt feels the proportions of the car were right for Europe. "Tall-cars have a lot more personality, and the high beltline gives the car a protective quality, which is something that you see in European hatchbacks. Their cars may be small, but they give you, through large side surfaces, the feel of being secure."

Painted a color called Aztec Yellow, the Pronto Cruizer had an exaggerated look to it. The cab was set back, the fenders and grille seemed larger than life, while the running boards, which flow smoothly into the fenders, were a distinct 1940s styling cue. The roof sported a fold-back canvas sunroof. A steeply raked rear hatch and larger rear wheels made the car look like it was ready to pounce.

Dave Smith, a 10-year Chrysler veteran and graduate of Detroit's Center for Creative Studies, designed an interior that was a blend of Art Deco with a techno feel. "Unlike the Japanese [cars], it has a European feel—functional, not trendy," he explains.

An aluminum finish was used on all functional interior areas like the instrument cluster, armrest, center stack, door handles, steering wheel, shifter knob, and shifter gate. Carbon fiber was used on items like the door map pockets, and the leather seat texture has a unique carbon fiber look to it.

The instruments were clustered in a pod behind the retro-styled three-spoke steering wheel with light-blue-colored faces that turned a deeper blue with the lights on. A

The PT Cruizer begat the production PT Cruiser above, a five-door tall wagon that defies categorization. The two versions are similar, except that the concept has a canvas roof and all-wheel drive. *Chrysler*

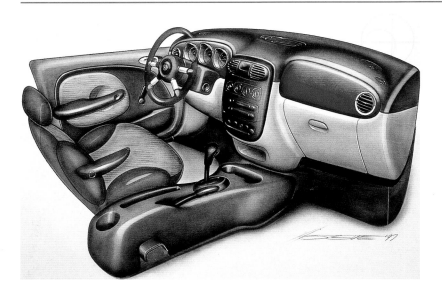

Sketch shows that retro cues extend inside PT Cruiser as well. Plastic inserts give the appearance of body-colored metal. *Chrysler*

screen for the on-board navigation system dominated the center stack, and three simple knobs controlled the heating and air conditioning system. In a light touch, the shift ball and the pedals were decorated with "happy faces."

The car was a hit at the Geneva auto show, though some British magazines sniffed that the look was somewhat similar to the legendary London Taxi. But more important, everyone who saw the Pronto Cruizer as an American hot rod retromobile "got it." That was in direct contrast to the VW New Beetle, which was taking America by storm, but not going gangbusters in Europe, particularly among Germans, who wondered why anyone would pay homage to the lowly Bug.

Meanwhile, as the PT44 was nearing completion, a show car and a production model were being secretly built for the 1999 North American International Auto Show. The press was briefed beforehand on the four concepts that were to "star" at the show, the Dodge Charger and Power Wagon, the Chrysler Citadel, and the Jeep Commander.

On Sunday, January 3, at Cobo Hall, disaster struck. A winter storm had buried Detroit in a foot of snow, cutting power for a time from the exhibition hall. After scrambling to find generators, the show went on, even as out-of-towners were stranded at the airport, some of them waiting as long as seven hours for their planes to dock at the gates.

After Bob Eaton had gone through the four concepts, each one coming out of a time machine with a projected feasible production date flashing above the door (the earliest being the Charger in 2004), out popped the PT Cruiser concept.

Slightly more conservative looking than the Pronto Cruizer, the PT Cruiser was a five-door with a more restrained grille and fenders. The touchdown point of the windshield was much farther forward and both the front windshield and rear hatch were less raked. Still, there was no mistaking the forward gesture of the car's proportions or the hot rod influence in the car's styling.

While it shared the look and a few key features like the roll-back canvas sunroof, this PT Cruiser had a different drivetrain—the company's 2.4-liter four-cylinder, which produced 150 horsepower. And the PT Cruiser concept was all-wheel drive.

The concept was put back into the "time machine" and the feasible production date read 2001. Out popped a nearly identical PT Cruiser, this one painted silver. Unlike the concept, it had no sunroof, was front-wheel drive only, but in almost every other respect, was identical to the concept car.

The other significant change was that the vehicle, which started out as a Plymouth Pronto, became the Chrysler PT Cruiser, foreshadowing the demise of the Plymouth nameplate. The PT was derived from the PT44 code name and was said to mean "Personal Transportation."

Nesbitt's hot rod shape from the Cruizer is equally at home on the five-door body. The drawing shows that the car was lowered and also emphasizes the forward gesture of the overall design. *Chrysler*

The finished car, while using the Prowler-inspired grille and promising to sell for a Plymouth-like base price of $16,000, used chromed door handles and the ornate Chrysler winged badge front and rear to convey a more upscale aura.

The interior carried on the Art Deco theme of the Pronto Cruizer. The instrument panel had two body-colored plastic inserts (that mimicked metal) on the dash front. The passenger side insert hid the airbag, while the driver's side had three instrument faces with chrome bezels set into it. The center stack also had a metal-like finish. On the manual-equipped PT Cruiser, the shifter was a chrome lever with a Bakelite knob, adding to the car's retro cues.

Like the Megane Scenic it was to compete with in Europe, the PT Cruiser had a flexible seating system. The rear seats folded down or could easily be removed, while the front passenger seat folded flat forward, allowing objects as long as eight feet to be carried inside the vehicle. A unique five-position parcel shelf in the back could be used to divide the cargo area behind the rear seat or even propped out the back with a drop-down leg as a table for use at tailgate parties.

While the simultaneous launch of concept car and production version was an industry first, it was the production model that got all the ink. Most of the show reports virtually ignored the gold all-wheel-drive concept.

Even before the vehicle was launched in March 2000 as a 2001 model, Chrysler's design staff was still working on PT Cruiser concepts. Yet another element in Chrysler's concept car strategy, to do one-off show cars of existing models, was played out in November at the 1999 Specialty Equipment Market Association (SEMA) show in Las Vegas. There, the GT Cruiser was shown. Even though the production vehicle was still nearly five months away from its official launch, the company was already promoting a new version.

The idea of doing the vehicle was to underscore its appeal to the youth market. "PT Cruiser already is difficult to categorize," Gale said at the GT Cruiser unveiling. "With GT Cruiser, we're showing the SEMA show participants—who are all about customizing and tuning—how one could take the PT Cruiser to the next level: lowered, with subtle design modifications and added power."

"We followed traditional customizing guidelines," adds Kenneth Carlson, senior designer in charge of GT Cruiser. "However, we applied a distinct modern design vocabulary to the modifications. Lowering the vehicle by one inch, by widening the track by two inches, gives it a mildly 'slammed' impression. We also removed the badges from the hood and deck and integrated the bumpers into the fascia. On GT Cruiser, the badges are incorporated in the grille and rear license plate brow, as you would see on a classic hot rod."

The GT Cruiser had a new front end with a smaller grille. An energy-absorbing fascia replaced the

Even before PT Cruiser was launched, Chrysler put together a supercharged concept called GT Cruiser. Note the smaller front grille, the bumper integrated into the fascia, and the lower secondary intake flanked by large driving lights. *Chrysler*

The two-door Panel Cruiser concept is the latest addition to the PT family. Though Chrysler hasn't committed to production plans, the Panel Cruiser was a star at the 2000 North American International Auto Show. *Chrysler*

traditional bumper and a secondary grille was added at the bottom and flanked by two large driving lights. On the rear of the vehicle, the badge with integrated latch was moved to the bottom of the hatch to give the rear end a cleaner look. An integrated body-colored rear bumper added to the streamlined look. The wheel flares were also larger, which helped accommodate the bigger 17-inch wheels shod with P215/50R-17 tires. The dual chrome exhaust tips underscored the sporty nature of the GT Cruiser.

Beneath the hood, the 2.4-liter four received a supercharger, which increased output to 200 horsepower and

225 ft-lb of torque. The engine was mated to a five-speed manual transmission from the Neon ACR club racing parts bin. The vehicle's lowered ride height and wider track came courtesy of ACR Koni/Mopar struts and upgraded sway bars.

Gale says the importance of the GT Cruiser was that it demonstrated "how this design can be individualized to suit anyone's taste."

But on a larger scale, it also demonstrated the total integration of the concept car mentality in Chrysler's production development process, from initial idea, through development, to even after the vehicle has been introduced.

FROM REALITY TO CONCEPT

While the focus for most of the concepts undertaken by Chrysler was clearly on future models, some fairly interesting ideas have been developed over time from existing models. Starting as far back as 1989 with the Dodge Dakota Sport and the 1990 Dodge Daytona R/T, Chrysler has tweaked and toyed with its production vehicles and put them out on the show circuit.

The Dakota Sport featured a longer hood to accommodate a V-8 engine, a longer cab and a modern interpretation of the traditional rumble seat with the rear glass sliding into the bulkhead which in turn folded backwards into the bed. The rear seatback, which was attached to the bulkhead, became the cushion for a rearward facing open-air bench.

The Daytona R/T was designed to pump some performance life into the Dodge division by showcasing all-wheel-drive technology and a new variable-nozzle turbocharger technology that was being tested on the company's 2.2-liter four-cylinder engine.

While there were numerous other packages, like Jeeps outfitted with rugged off-road packages and even a convertible Cherokee, three vehicles that best illustrate how far concept car thinking can take an existing product are the Chrysler Pacifica, Dodge Caravan R/T, and Plymouth Voyager XG minivans.

The one unqualified hit in Chrysler's portfolio that helped solve the company's first financial crisis is the minivan. To mark the 15th anniversary of this vehicle in 1998, three show cars were built to hint at the future of this stalwart of Chrysler's line-up.

"While it's our policy not to discuss future product, I can tell you that there is still an opportunity for us to push the styling envelope for future minivans," says John Herlitz. "We aren't even close to exhausting our styling and packaging ideas for adding excitement and function to minivans."

Fresh thinking, though, wouldn't hurt. In the late 1990s, minivan sales peaked at about 1.5 million units annually, of which Chrysler's share was just under 40 percent. But SUVs are taking an increasing share of the family vehicle market. New thinking is needed to break the minivan out of the "mom-mobile" stigma. The challenge is to get people to drive minivans because they want to, not because they have to.

The most radical of the three designs was the Chrysler Pacifica, a limousine wrapped in a minivan skin. Based on the Chrysler Town & Country minivan, the inspiration for its execution came from aviation.

Dodge Dakota Sport V-8 was one of the first Chrysler concepts to be pulled off a production vehicle. It featured a rear bench in the extended cab that could be flipped over into the bed to create a rumble seat. *Chrysler*

To commemorate the industry-leading Chrysler minivan's 15th anniversary, three concept vehicles show the future potential of these family workhorses. They are the Chrysler Pacifica, left foreground, Dodge Caravan R/T, right, and the Plymouth XG. *Bill Delaney*

"Our Pacifica concept was inspired by the luxury and convenience offered in executive jet travel," says Neil Walling. "We wanted Pacifica to bring the benefits of executive jet travel down to earth, into the minivan, and onto the road."

The front end of the Pacifica was restyled with an egg-crate grille that mimicked the look of the LHS and rounder headlamps with separate projector beam bulbs. Fog lamps were integrated into a chin spoiler. The raised roof on the Pacifica featured a center skylight, while to the side were handy storage bins accessed from the interior on the driver's side and from the exterior on the passenger's side.

The rear seats were positioned to the rear of the cabin to provide the room needed for the power foot rests. Two additional passengers could be accommodated on fold-down jump seats that were attached to the back of the front buckets.

A special golf bag rack was fitted to the rear of the van and could hold up to four sets of clubs. Other luxury features included overhead aircraft-style lighting, a drop-down video screen, and fine wood and leather accents.

Sure to shake up the image of the mom-mobile was the performance-oriented Dodge Caravan R/T. Fitted with 18-inch wheels, an Autostick sequential-shift automatic, and a 225-horsepower 3.5-liter V-6, this short wheelbase minivan looked as ready to tackle a slalom course as it was to pick up the kids from soccer practice.

The Caravan R/T, painted Viper Red, had a clean, sporty front fascia that incorporated driving lights, a red ram medallion floating in the middle of a blacked-out grille, blacked-out moldings, mirrors, and two hood scoops similar to the Viper's. The door handles had a metallic finish with large R/T decals and five-spoke mag wheels completing the look.

Inside, the designers used brushed aluminum accents for the vents, door latches, instrument panel, and pedals. The steering wheel was wrapped in leather and the leather sport buckets had the red R/T logo embroidered on the headrests. The entire floor was covered in black rubber with a raised tread texture, making the vehicle easy to clean. Additional storage was offered in an overhead console and dual center consoles, one for front seat passengers, the other for those seated in the rear.

Dodge Daytona R/T sports additional body cladding to highlight the fact that a 2.2-liter four-cylinder with variable nozzle turbocharger beats beneath its hood. *Chrysler*

The Plymouth Voyager XG was aimed at people with active outdoor lifestyles, be it snowboarding or street luge. "We built the Plymouth Voyager XG concept minivan for the adventure-seeking mountain-biking, trail-riding, ocean-surfing individual who has a lot of equipment and is always on the go," says Ralph Sarotte, general manager of the minivan platform. "We hope to expand the minivan market segment by attracting a new generation of minivan buyers."

The Voyager XG was powered by a 2.5-liter turbodiesel mated to a five-speed manual transmission. The diesel was chosen for its 28 miles per gallon performance, which meant greater range and less money spent on fuel.

Painted in Starbrite Silver Metallic, the Voyager XG had a high-tech, expressive look. Actual changes to the exterior were minimal, except for the custom paint, large decals, and the five-spoke 17-inch wheels, which were borrowed from the Prowler.

The interior featured four captain's chairs in taupe and finished with a high-tech fabric that has a woven metal look to it. Ample storage was provided by a series of cargo nets strategically placed on the backs of the seats, on the rear headliner and inside quarter panels, on the doors, and even between the seats.

Other features included a power canvas sunroof that opened nearly the entire length of the vehicle and a removable storage pod that could be used as a storage drawer or an ice chest.

"Plymouth Voyager XG is a keeper of stuff," Sarotte said at the vehicle's debut. "When you get off work, there's no need to go home. You can store your stuff securely in the back and make a quick getaway to the beach or trails."

DAIMLERCHRYSLER DAYS

It took over 10 years for Chrysler to lift itself from its reputation as the weakest of the U.S. Big Three to a profitable dynamo on the cutting edge of automotive design. But it took only 17 minutes for the idea of a trans-Atlantic merger with Daimler-Benz to take hold and less than six months for it to become a reality.

Daimler-Benz Chairman Jurgen Schrempp made no secret of the fact that one of the things that drew him to Chrysler Chairman Bob Eaton's office that January afternoon in 1998 was the American company's design skills embodied in both concept and production cars.

The question that emerged was would Chrysler continue to be at the leading edge of design under the new arrangement?

The naysayers pointed to the retirements of Bob Lutz, Francois Castaing, Tom Stallkamp, and Neil Walling, who headed advanced design. Key members of the crack public relations staff had defected to GM, and other product development types had gone to Ford. People free to work under a carefully developed system that stressed flexibility and speed had spelled success for Chrysler. Take the people away, change the system, and what's left?

After initial studies in combining the two staffs, DaimlerChrysler management reversed course and decided to let Chrysler and Mercedes-Benz function as autonomous units. Jim Holden, who headed up sales and marketing, was promoted to president replacing Tom Stallkamp, who took early retirement after struggling to combine the two companies. The most important move, however, was the consolidation of product development and design under Tom Gale, who for the second time in his career was called upon to be keeper of the flame.

Dave Holls, who served as design director for General Motors and worked under design chiefs all the way back to the legendary Harley Earl, says: "Tom Gale has been more influential than you can imagine. He set a standard over there at Chrysler that not only we in the United States but the whole world had to watch. He had a wonderful

Surface development of the 300 Hemi C adds more muscle to the body. The leading edge curves down through the front of the vehicle, giving the headlamps a hooded look. *John Lamm*

Java is the first concept car to blend Mercedes-Benz components with a Chrysler design. The shape, penned before the merger, stresses the idea of minimal front and rear overhang. With the wheels pushed so far out to the corners, it was an ideal candidate for the Mercedes A-Class platform, which has similar proportions. *Chrysler*

friend in Bob Lutz, who helped him achieve a lot of this stuff. But Tom still had to do it."

The key to Gale's success has been his rapport with his subordinates. "Every design operation is operated a little differently and has different people who run the place," Holls explains. "At General Motors we had dynamos like Harley Earl and Bill Mitchell. In his own gentle, quiet way, Tom was able to achieve as much as those guys did in their time. I think Chrysler set the standards for our era now."

Gale says that while he will greatly miss Walling, he was happy to recruit Freeman Thomas, the VW and Audi designer who helped create the New Beetle and Audi TT, as his replacement for vice president of advanced design.

And Gale's core team, which includes John Herlitz and Trevor Creed, has remained largely intact. How well

Gale's design team functions in this new environment was revealed in the Java, a small urban car unveiled at the Frankfurt Motor Show in September 1999, and the four vehicles unveiled at the 2000 North American International Auto Show. This crop included a new Viper, the 300 Hemi C convertible, the Jeep Varsity, and the Dodge Maxxcab pickup.

Java represents Gale's further evolution of the cab forward theme to even more radical extremes. The cabin has grown to where the vehicle is almost a one-box design with minimal front and rear overhang.

"Java was done in fiberglass before the merger," Gale says. "It was the front overhang that I wanted and it was a wakeup call to our own people and caused them to start to reach." He called his new look "Passenger Priority Design," which maximized interior volume relative to the exterior dimensions.

Java's interior package was nearly the same as the PT Cruiser displayed next to it, and yet Java stood nearly 20 inches shorter with an overall length of just 148 inches. "This tall architecture and panoramic seating for driver and passengers allows for higher H-points to give them more of an in-control feeling compared to other small cars," Gale explains. "In fact, the rear passengers are sitting higher than the front passengers, creating an automotive form of theater seating."

The look reinforced Chrysler's brand heritage by using the winged badge and rectangular egg-crate grille opening. The creases in the shape recalled the 300M.

What made Java unusual, though, was the use of the Mercedes A-Class platform. Gale went to Jurgen Hubbert, head of Mercedes-Benz product development, and asked to use the A-Class as a means of demonstrating the synergies that exist between the two companies.

Kevin Verduyn, senior design manager at Pacifica, says: "Java was a logical follow-up to previous design studies such as Pronto and CCV. We were looking for the most efficient yet stylish way to move four people around in a sub-four-meter car. We also had the freedom to use

European-based DaimlerChrysler components such as the powertrain, transaxle, and the suspension." The use of these off-the-shelf components also speeded development of a running show car, a must in Gale's book.

An 80-horsepower, 1.4-liter four-cylinder engine mated to a five-speed manual transmission powered Java. It had a 98.3-inch wheelbase and used the A-Class independent suspension, which combined wishbones, MacPherson struts, double-tube shocks, and a stabilizer bar up front and trailing links with coil springs, monotube shocks, and stabilizer bar in the rear. True to show car form, Java was shod with 18-inch wheels with P185/50R-18 rubber. Java was capable of a top speed of 105 miles per hour and could accelerate from 0-62 miles per hour in 12.9 seconds.

Java was important because Gale believes it represented some middle ground in the rhetoric surrounding the merger or, as it's viewed by others, acquisition of Chrysler by Daimler-Benz. Opinions on the structure of the organization have ranged from totally combining operations to continuing to share nothing between entities.

"Somewhere in there is the right mix," Gale says. "The last thing we would want to do is denigrate a brand. When we took over AMC, we were more protective than Jeep. None of us want to be hammered for being the one that screwed it up. We feel the same way about Mercedes, Chrysler, Dodge, and Jeep. We are putting a much stronger face on the products." At the same time, Gale believes that there are underskin components that can be shared.

The strong face on product was evident in the four cars unveiled in Detroit—Viper GTSR, Chrysler 300 Hemi C, Dodge Maxxcab pickup, and Jeep Varsity.

Unlike 1999, when the theme was the environment, Gale says there was a conscious decision to do cars that were closer to production reality inside and out. "We could do the environmental theme again, but then it gets expected. This year is similar to 1996 when we did the Intrepid ESX, which was the Intrepid and the LHX, which was the LHS. We haven't decided to do all

The Java's interior shows touches taken from previous Chrysler show car icons like the Chronos. Note that the instrument panel has the look of an expensive chronograph. Light-colored wood accents and brushed aluminum give this entry-level hatchback the feel of an upscale luxury model. *Chrysler*

As this sketch shows, Viper GTSR has a much bolder face than the current GTS Coupe. *Chrysler*

From above, note the separate hood and fenders, which replace the single clamshell piece on earlier Vipers. There's much more tension in the shape along with a subtle Coke-bottle effect. *John Lamm*

Inspired by the Viper's racing successes, the GTSR sports a huge rear wing, front aerodynamic splitter, and roof air intake. *John Lamm*

four, but when we look back on this, when you see our cars in the future, you're going to say this is where you first saw them."

The star of the show, naturally, was Viper GTSR. Eleven years had passed since it first burst on the scene as a concept, yet the 2000 version, like the original, also gave a hint of what the future holds. The inspirations for the show car were the GTS-R Le Mans and FIA GT-2 champion racecar, but Gale stresses that this is "a street-legal, all-out performance car."

Based on the current Viper drivetrain, the show car's V-10 was tuned to produce 500 horsepower and 500 ft-lb of torque. The wheelbase was extended three inches, with

the rear wheels moved aft. Racing-inspired aerodynamic bits included the front splitter, side skirts, high wing, roof-mounted air intake (to cool the cabin and rear differential) and underbody fencing.

The car had a bolder face, with a larger, more open grille, huge driving lights built into the fascia, and wider headlamps with a stronger projector-beam look to them. The one-piece clamshell hood had given way to a more conventional design that featured separate fenders and a rear-hinged hood. The engine had dry sump oiling which helped lower the hoodline. Gale says the switch to separate fenders gave the car a better defined and more powerful shape from the driver's perspective. The entire body was executed in carbon fiber.

The sides of the Viper sported large side scoops and a round intake for rear brake cooling. The entire body of the

The Viper GTSR has an all-new interior, which includes mounting auxiliary gauges in a pod running alongside the center stack. Particular attention was paid to placement, so that these instruments would not be obstructed by the steering wheel. The center vents have the look of a butterfly valve, while the shift knob is polished chrome. *John Lamm*

Viper Coupe was exaggerated to make it look larger than life. In production, the side scoops wouldn't be as deep nor would the rear body extension be as long as the show car's.

Inside, the cabin had a cockpit feel due to a binnacle that swept over and down through the center console, incorporating additional instrumentation as well as the center stack controls for the radio and ventilation system. While the rear fencing might be a bolt-on option from the Mopar catalog, the top air intake was intended to be production-ready.

Along with a facelift for Dodge's flagship Viper, Chrysler may have finally found its icon in the 300 Hemi C concept car. This four-passenger ragtop was equipped with a prototype 5.7-liter pushrod V-8 with hemispherical combustion chambers. Unlike the original Hemi, though, this new-age muscle motor was made of aluminum and had twin-spark coil-on-plug ignition. The rebirth of the

Hemi took on added significance in light of Chrysler's decision to return to NASCAR racing in 2001.

The rear-drive 300 Hemi C was based on the LH platform, but the five-link independent rear suspension employed Mercedes S-Class uprights, which also showed the synergies that exist in the new company.

"The 300 Hemi C is close to the kind of proportions and the kind of execution you could expect to someday see," Gale notes. The car measured 198 inches in overall length and rode on a 116-inch wheelbase. The fabric top was automatic and Gale says the daylight opening was made wide with a thin C-pillar look. "We wanted a car that looked just as elegant with the top up," Gale adds.

Detailing like the flared wheel arches and fairings behind the rear seat headrests lend a classic air to the 300 Hemi C. *John Lamm*

The 300 Hemi C had a front fascia that was similar in look to the 300M with fluted headlamps flanking a small grille. The front end had almost a hooded appearance. The front wheels were flared wide to give the car a muscular stance. Handsome side air vents were used to break up the long dash-to-axle ratio. Inside, the leather-clad interior sported wood and chrome accents and white-faced instruments inspired by upscale watches.

Just when automakers were rushing to build cars with SUV-like characteristics, Jeep took the wraps off an SUV that was supposed to act like a car. The Varsity featured the ride height and lower body styling of a Jeep, yet the greenhouse had the elegant arch of a four-door sedan. Powered by a 3.5-liter V-6 driving all four wheels, the Varsity was dubbed "an urban adventure concept." The front end had round headlamps, which flanked the traditional seven-slat Jeep grille opening. The hood was recessed from the A-pillar giving the Varsity the look of a utility. Reinforcing that rugged look were traditional Jeep cues such as rectangular wheelwell openings and lower body cladding. Ever protective of the franchise, Varsity was designed to see if there's a market for such a crossover vehicle that wouldn't alienate Jeep traditionalists.

Although the Varsity sports a rugged face, the rounder edges on the greenhouse soften the overall impact of the vehicle. Even though it is relatively slab sided, sharp creases and the squared-off wheel wells add to the Varsity's appeal. *John Lamm*

The Dodge Maxxcab was a crew cab pickup that used the Java's Passenger Priority Design philosophy of a short front overhang while maximizing the cabin space.

"This is carving out a dramatic new proportion on trucks," Gale says. "The Maxxcab pickup was to trucks what we did with some of the sedans a long time ago. Truck architecture has evolved classically over the years. Nobody has really gone back and said, 'Let's turn everything over, take it apart, and put it back together in some different way.' It's like a kid building with Lincoln Logs; you don't always have to keep building the same house."

With its pug-nose styling and large passenger cabin, the Maxxcab presented a totally different proportion on a truck platform. While others were doing sport-utility vehicles with pickup beds added on the back, the Maxxcab looked more like a minivan with a pickup bed.

The Dodge Maxxcab tries to do for trucks what cab forward did for cars. The passenger cabin is almost minivan-like in proportion. *John Lamm*

These four vehicles were further evidence that out-of-the-box thinking has survived at Chrysler and that the importance of concept cars was not being taken less seriously under the new management structure. It will be business as usual. That's because, Gale concludes, "Concept cars are the face of Chrysler."

Though the interior has all the bells and whistles of a show car, such as a pop-up computer screen, it's interesting to note that the dash has almost a car or minivan feel to it, thanks to the cab forward architecture. *John Lamm*

INDEX

Alternative Engine Taskforce (AET), 38, 39, 43
American Motors Corporation (AMC), 10, 14
Andrea Doria [?], 28
Austin-Healey Sprite, 58
Automobili Lamborghini, 10
Automotive News, 99
Barris, George, 28
Batmobile, 28
Big Shot, 21, 57
Bott, Dick, 40
Buick Riviera, 28
Buick Silver Arrow I, 31
Buick Silver Arrow, 28
Buick Wildcat, 28, 32
Buick Y-Job, 27
Carlson, Kenneth, 131
Castaing, Francois, 11, 13, 14, 23, 29, 38, 39, 79, 80, 91–93, 95–97, 104, 126, 137
Chevrolet Corvette Manta Ray, 28
Chevrolet Corvette Sting Ray, 28
Chevrolet Corvette, 28, 29
Chevrolet Nomad, 28
Chrysler 300 Hemi C, 138, 140–142
Chrysler 300, 64, 66, 67, 108
Chrysler 300M, 101, 117, 121, 142
Chrysler Airflow, 27, 29
Chrysler Atlantic, 14, 69–71, 73
Chrysler Chronos, 28, 73, 74, 117, 121
Chrysler Cirrus, 33, 43, 44
Chrysler Citadel, 106–108, 116–121
Chrysler d'Elegance, 28, 73
Chrysler GT Cruiser, 123, 131–133
Chrysler Imperial LeBaron Newport, 27
Chrysler Imperial, 14, 35
Chrysler JA cars, 43
Chrysler Java, 136, 138, 139, 142
Chrysler LHS, 101
Chrysler LHX, 102, 103, 140
Chrysler LRT, 38
Chrysler Millennium, 15, 16, 18, 19, 21, 31
Chrysler Navaho, 9, 17
Chrysler New Yorker, 35, 101
Chrysler Pacifica, 134, 135, 138
Chrysler Panel Cruiser, 133
Chrysler Patriot, 90, 92, 93
Chrysler Phaeton, 14, 71, 72
Chrysler Portofino, 9–14, 17, 18, 21, 31, 127
Chrysler PT Cruiser, 46, 47, 65, 123, 126–131, 138
Chrysler TC Coupe, 18, 19
Chrysler TEVan, 42
Chrysler Thunderbolt, 27, 28, 68, 69
Chrysler Turbine, 28, 30
Chrysler Voyager III, 45, 46

Composite Concept Vehicle (CCV), 92, 94, 95, 97, 105
Crain, Jack, 73
Credit Suisse, 40
Creed, Trevor, 81, 82, 84, 113, 118, 138
Cunningham, Briggs, 14
Daimler-Benz, 75, 137, 140
Dehner, Joe, 109
DeTomaso, Alejandro, 18
Diamond-Star, 35
Dodge Caravan R/T, 134, 135
Dodge Charger R/T, 107, 109, 110, 116, 117
Dodge Charger, 55, 106, 108, 109
Dodge CNG Charger R/T, 108
Dodge Copperhead, 56, 57, 59–61
Dodge Dakota Sport, 134
Dodge Dakota, 37, 88
Dodge Daytona R/T, 134, 135
Dodge Daytona, 35
Dodge Dynasty, 35
Dodge Intrepid ESX, 102–104, 140
Dodge Intrepid ESX2, 105
Dodge Intrepid, 18, 21, 65
Dodge LH, 17
Dodge LRT, 37
Dodge Maxxcab, 138, 140, 142, 143
Dodge Monaco, 35
Dodge Neon Aviat, 45, 46, 54, 91
Dodge Neon Expresso, 46, 47, 54
Dodge Neon, 33, 38–40, 47, 54, 125
Dodge Omni, 36
Dodge Power Wagon, 106, 107, 111–117
Dodge Ram truck, 65
Dodge Ram VTS, 51
Dodge Shadow, 35
Dodge Sidewinder, 88
Dodge Spirit, 35
Dodge Stratus, 33, 43, 65
Dodge T-Rex, 88, 89
Dodge Venom, 54–58
Dodge Viper Coupe, 72
Dodge Viper GTS Coupe, 14, 50, 51
Dodge Viper GTS, 55
Dodge Viper GTS-R, 51, 52, 139, 140
Dodge Viper Roadster, 72
Dodge Viper, 19–25, 31, 33, 35, 38, 54, 57, 65, 67, 117, 138
Dong, Leong C., 88
Durfey, Craig, 17, 23
Eagle Jazz, 98, 100, 101
Eagle Optima, 34, 36
Eagle Premier, 35
Eagle Summit, 36
Eagle Talon, 35

Eagle Vision, 101
Earl, Harley, 27, 137, 138
Eaton, Bob, 51, 52, 99, 123, 128, 137
Electric Power Inter-urban Commuter (EPIC), 40–43, 91, 106
Exner, Virgil, 28
External Breathing Direction Injection (EBDI), 38
Ford GT90, 99
Ford Nucleon, 28
Ford Taurus, 29, 99, 100
Ford Thunderbird, 29, 99
Ford, Henry, II, 18
Gale, Tom, 9, 11, 13–18, 21, 23, 29–33, 43, 45, 46, 52–55, 57, 68, 69, 75, 87, 89, 97, 100, 101, 102, 104, 107, 108, 110, 116, 125, 133, 137–143
Gardner, Glenn, 91
Giugiaro, Giorgetto, 121
Goldfinger, 45
Gulfstream Aviation, 10
Guts: The Seven Laws of Business that Made Chrysler the World's Hottest Car Company, 35, 77
Harris, Steve, 11
Herlitz, John, 11, 54, 56, 134, 138
Holden, Jim, 126, 137
Holls, Dave, 137, 138
Hot Shot, 21, 57
Hubbach, Bob, 69
Hubbert, Jurgen, 138
Iacocca, Lee, 9, 10, 17, 18, 29, 37, 51, 52, 91
ItalDesign, 121
Jeep Commander, 106, 108, 114, 116, 118–121
Jeep Concept 1, 77, 80
Jeep Dakar, 84–87
Jeep Ecco, 76, 78–81
Jeep Grand Cherokee, 87, 111
Jeep Icon, 81, 82
Jeep KJ, 87
Jeep Varsity, 138, 142
Jeep Wagoneer 2000, 78, 79
Jeep WJ, 87
Jeep Wrangler, 78, 81, 84, 85
Jeep XJ, 87
Jeep, 10
Jeepster, 82–85
Jordan, Chuck, 45
Kerkorian, Kirk, 52
Kowaleski, Tom, 11
Laster, Robert, 82
Liberty, 91, 95–97, 105
Lincoln Futura, 28
Lincoln L2K, 99
Lutz, Robert A., 11, 13, 14, 16–18, 21, 23, 29–31, 35, 38–40, 45, 46, 51, 52, 54,

65–67, 69, 72, 75, 77, 80, 85, 87, 99, 101, 107, 112, 124, 126
Mercedes-Benz, 137, 138
Metalcrafters, 13, 23
Mitchell, Bill, 138
Monteverdi High Speed, 65–67
Monteverdi, Peter, 14, 65, 66
Moore, Mike, 82
Moore, Tom, 91, 95, 96
Nesbitt, Bryan, 126, 127, 131
Oldsmobile Aerotech, 29
Plymouth Acclaim, 35
Plymouth Backpack, 47
Plymouth Horizon, 36
Plymouth Howler, 89
Plymouth Laser, 35
Plymouth Pronto Cruiser, 123, 127, 128, 130
Plymouth Pronto Spyder, 57–59, 62, 63, 119
Plymouth Pronto, 122, 124–126
Plymouth Prowler Woodward Avenue edition, 55
Plymouth Prowler, 33, 53–56, 65
Plymouth Speedster, 33
Plymouth Sundance, 35
Plymouth Voyager XG, 135
Plymouth XG, 134
Pontiac Banshee, 28
Renault 25, 35
Renault Espace, 40
Renault, 123
Reynard, Adrian, 92, 95
Robertson, Bernard, 116
Rosen brothers, 93
Rundels, Jon, 59, 89
Schrempp, Jurgen, 137
Schuttera, Christopher, 89
Shelby, Carroll, 21, 23
Shikado, Osamu, 73, 121
Sjoberg, Roy, 23
Sling Shot, 17, 21, 57
Smith, Dave, 128
Sowinski, Steve, 114
Sperlich, Hal, 21, 57
Stallkamp, Tom, 29, 137
Syntroleum, 116
Telnack, Jack, 29, 99
Theodore, Chris, 126
Thomas, Freeman, 138
Tremont, Tom, 58
Tremulis, Alex, 27, 28
Tsuchiya, Akino, 121
Tucker, 27
Verduyn, Kevin, 138
Walling, Neil, 23, 45, 54, 56, 101, 108, 121, 125, 127, 135, 137, 138